CW00507819

To Olivia and my family for al
not be where I am today withc

Table of Contents

Preface: Picture This

Chapter 1: A Skill not a Ticked Box

Chapter 2: The Starting Point

Chapter 3: How to Pick the right story

Chapter 4.1: How to Analyse a Story - Micro-focus

Chapter 4.2: How to Analyse a Story - The Broader Picture

Chapter 5: How to Discuss a Story

Preface: Picture This

I reach out for a glass of water to calm my nerves. I'm sitting in front of a partner, and it's my final interview for a Training Contract. The interview is going well; minus some minor slip-ups, I've somehow managed to provide a decent answer to all their questions. Then I look up, waiting for the next question. They look at me, and after a brief pause, ask me the dreaded question. The one I'd hoped would never come up, the one I probably should have prepared to answer.

"So..have you been reading the news lately? Why don't you tell us about a story that caught your attention and how you think it could impact our clients?"

I go blank for a second. Are those three questions in one? So not only did they ask me that horrible question, but they multiplied it by three?! I take yet another sip of water to try and relax. I pause and desperately try to remember a BBC news article I glanced at the night before.

After a few endless minutes, I utter nervously..." I read about Brexit..". Great. Brexit, I think to myself. You've just picked out one of the most complicated, far-reaching, and unoriginal topics in the world.

I stare at the interviewer and try to grapple together a series of chaotic points about its impact on trade and the future of the UK economy (I know, ten points for originality!). I explain how this story caught my attention as an international student in the UK and then stop. That was horrible, but at least it's done.

The interviewer looks at me and asks, "And what about our clients?". Fantastic. I even forgot one of their questions. I anxiously piece together a few superficial and general points about the impact of Brexit on international clients and a potential demand shift to EU-based firms and then stop again.

Overall that probably lasted 4 minutes, including all my unnecessary pauses. I knew my answers were not good. They lacked analysis, structure, and application.

A week later, I received a call from the firm to say I did not make it to the vacation scheme (the next step in the Training Contract application).

When I asked for feedback, I was told, amongst other things, that my commercial awareness answer should have been more detailed.

At that moment, I realised that commercial awareness mattered, and just glancing at news stories would not cut it.

There and then, I decided it would become my top priority going forward.

Why does it matter?

If you had asked me why or even if commercial awareness mattered five years ago, I would have answered with a blank "what?".

I had no idea what commercial awareness was, and even after being explained what it was, I could not understand how it related to my wanting to be a lawyer.

I always thought a lawyer was supposed to focus on the law. Commercial awareness was something for accountants or people interested in finance. Surely a client would not come to a lawyer asking for commercial advice, right?? Wrong!

The role of a lawyer is naturally that of a commercial advisor. Legal advice is based on commercial thinking.

How much would this cost the client? How would option A benefit them more than option B? How could this solution protect their business? The questions are endless.

I often compare the need for commercial awareness to the need to understand math. When studying the Pythagorean theorem, you'd wonder when the hell would I even use it. You don't realise you subconsciously use it every day. Whether it's to pick a shorter route to a destination or to pick the size of a new TV, the Pythagorean theorem is there for you. (And this comes from someone who always had a "complicated" relationship with maths, so I would happily do without it).

Likewise, it is undeniable that commercial awareness is a far-reaching concept. You instinctively apply commercial awareness daily, whether you're buying a cheese toastie for £1 less at a different store or buying a new energy drink you saw in an ad.

As shown in my brief story earlier, employers need people who understand how the commercial world works and not people who wing it. This book will share all I have learned about commercial awareness over the past four years through my studies, work, and growing The Business Update. It will outline theories, strategies, and practical resources which assisted me in understanding what commercial awareness is.

I hope that you will be able to pick out some valuable notions from this book that will assist you in becoming more commercially aware.

So thank you for choosing to read this book! Now let's find out what Commercial Awareness is and how we can use it to ace our interviews!

Chapter 1: A Skill not a Ticked Box

The great art of learning is to understand but little at a time. - John Locke

Breaking down a concept into manageable chunks has always been the best way for me to understand it. So why not apply this to commercial awareness, which in itself is potentially one of the most confusing and popular buzzwords in the graduate recruitment sector?

What is Commerciality?

Let's start with the commercial part of the equation. A quick search on Google won't be of much help here. It'll bring up way too many results which will confuse you even more. Commerciality in itself is a hugely broad concept that encompasses a disproportionate amount of topics.

So let's boil it down. In the context of commercial awareness, I interpret commerciality as a sense for business. Now, this will probably raise even more questions; most commonly, what do you mean by business?

I find that the best way to understand this is to visualise yourself as the CEO of a company.

Learning Example

In our example, you'll be the **CEO of Chipmunk Carrots**, a company focused on providing chipmunk-shaped carrot snacks around the world.

As a CEO, you'll most likely be focused on the needs of key parties. These are the business, the clients, and the stakeholders. When considering these needs you'll inevitably consider the external forces at play. These will be events in the local and global economy that will affect your key parties to answer threats and identify opportunities.

- So say you source your carrots from the Netherlands, what would you think and do if a series of storms destroyed the crops for the first half of the year?

- If you wanted to expand your business profits, how could you benefit from the surge in demand for vegan products?

- If a competitor began to copy your popular chip-munk-shaped carrots what would you do? (Yes - this is a bit farfetched but play along!)

I have found that this simple exercise forces me to become more analytical and consequently more commercial. The great thing about this strategy is that it can be deployed in any instance. If you read a story about Company X shutting 100 stores, place yourself as the CEO and think like a CEO. Think *commercially* about the key parties and the impact of both internal and external forces on your company. This will help you grasp with more confidence what is meant by commerciality.

Awareness is the wrong word

Now onto part two of our mysterious concept. Let me start by saying that **Awareness** is a questionable term.

As defined in the Cambridge dictionary, Awareness is the *"knowledge that something exists, or understanding of a situation or subject at present based on information or experience"*.

I always found that being *aware* of something does not necessarily mean that you *understand* it to the point you could explain it to a 5-year-old. For example, I may be aware of stock options derivatives, but I would not know how to explain them clearly.

The way I see it, **Awareness** comes in three rising levels. These can be briefly summarised as per the below:

- **Low Awareness**: Read a news notification and skim the news story

- **Medium Awareness**: Read the original story in full and two articles related to it and think about its impact on one key party

- **High Awareness**: Read all the above, analyse the impact on key parties, plot trends on framework template, and fill in news analysis structure

An individual with low and medium awareness focuses simply on what is readily available, i.e. what can be read on a news article even if to different extents. For an individual with High Awareness, these articles are merely a starting point. They focus on what is not written and come up with their own analysis.

5 Pillars of the Commercial Mindset

To build on the levels of awareness, we can think of five key areas that define the commercial mindset. These are skills and concepts which we can focus on developing to reach a high level of awareness. And the great thing is that this book will provide you with techniques and suggestions on how to do this!

Awareness

Yes, I know I just made a big point about *Awareness* being the wrong term for us to focus on in our journey to becoming more commercial. However, it still is an undeniable first step in the process.

This is the discovery stage. To discover stories, we need to be aware of what is happening in the world. This is relatively a simple skill to build as it involves actions as simple as opening your favourite news app daily or watching the news channel on TV for 10 minutes.

So, in short, be open to stories. It's easy to switch off when the news comes up as they tend to be quite dry and often filled with jargon. But try to make an effort and promise yourself ten uninterrupted minutes of attention. This will allow you to pick up on crucial concepts, which you will link up to different stories and trends you hear about the next day.

Analysis

Our second *pillar* is Analysis. Once we hear about a story on the news, we need to build on that Awareness through our analysis. This can come in varying levels of intensity. Don't worry. You don't need to spend hours analysing every time you see a news notification pop up on your phone!

However, if the story you become aware of is of particular interest to you, then why not spend a bit more time analysing it? If you think it's not as relevant, then still try to give it a quick read. Read both the article and maybe some suggested stories. This may allow you to discover some unexpected details that you can link up to your interests.

We will go through suggested methods for analysing stories at varying degrees of intensity later in the book. For now, just know that this stage requires you to be proactive. Awareness can occur with no action from you as you get hit by a news notification on your phone. For Analysis, it is up to you to open the story up, read it and take notes. How far are you willing to go?

Framework

This Pillar builds off our Analysis phase. The framework is a concept that I use to create links between stories to observe the bigger picture in the news.

One of the critical aspects of our Analysis models, which you will hear about in the book, is identifying *Trends*. This is an essential skill for anyone looking to move from a simple descriptive story explanation to a fully-fledged analytical discussion.

Identifying a Framework in our analysis of a story forces us to think Analytically. This lets us go beyond what is written in the article in front of us. You have to take the *initiative* to consider what stories you could link this current one to and what they tell you about the overall market movements.

The most significant improvement in my commercial analysis came when I stopped seeing stories as independent blocks and began to see them as small parts of large puzzles. At times, it may be harder to identify frameworks, but you will rarely find stories wholly unaffected by other stories or trends.

Dig deeper and see what you can find. The answer may be in front of everyone's eyes, but only some can see it.

Engagement

Did someone mention *Initiative*? Yes - it's back again. An essential part of becoming more commercial is your level of **engagement**.

We have all been there. We open up an article from a well-known news source and instantly switch off. The article is way too long, and in the first two sentences, there are 3 or 4 words you've never heard before. At that point, I used to choose what seemed like the obvious choice. Close the app and go on Instagram.

And those are the moments I want to focus on to strengthen your engagement.

Let's not pretend. Developing your commercial awareness can be complicated, tedious, and tiring, especially when the only time you have to catch up with stories is in between work or studies.

It boils down to how committed *you* are to becoming more commercially aware and this is a pervasive theme among all five pillars.

In the next chapter, we will consider building systems to develop habits that make improving your engagement levels a breeze.

Start by thinking, how much time and effort are you willing to put in? Are you ready to push further when you open an article full of jargon or complicated concepts?

Simplification

"If you can't explain it to a six-year-old, you don't understand it yourself" - Albert Einstein.

I have to agree with Albert on this one. If you fully understand something you should be able to explain it to a child in a way that makes sense for them. I find this is a brilliant way to practice your delivery and discussion skills.

This is something we will evaluate heavily in coming chapters as it is fundamental for us to be able to move from an analysis on paper to an in-person discussion.

This is the art of simplification. You don't need jargon to sound commercial. You need to know what it means and how *you* can explain it. Partly because the awkwardness of explaining derivatives after spending 7 minutes discussing a story focused on them is pretty overwhelming. (Based on a true story? Potentially, yes)

So if the article you're reading doesn't simplify concepts, take on the responsibility. Read the article and look up what all that jargon means but don't copy the definition from Investopedia. Think about it and put it in your own words in a way that makes sense for you and a six-year-old.

Simplification is the last of our pillars because it occurs when we have thoroughly analysed and understood concepts and stories. It is a vital part of the process as these simplified explanations are what sticks in our minds. Do not disregard it. Always try to make commercial topics six-year-old-friendly.

Last Thoughts

It is easy to fall into the trap of thinking that commercial awareness is just a box to tick. Something that once checked off by reading a story can be forgotten. I used to fall into this mindset because it's the easy way out. It's easy to say, "I read two articles on the FT yesterday, so I feel commercially aware for my interview tomorrow".

This leads most of us to limit ourselves to a state of Low and Medium awareness at most. It takes effort to push through and enter the High Awareness level, which will provide you with the most rewards.

In the next chapter, we will look at how to set up *Systems* that will allow you to develop your Awareness level to become a High Awareness Individual and build on our Five Pillars of Commercial Awareness.

Learning Points & Actions

At the end of each chapter, I will provide you with a series of Learning Points and Actions that you can build on the knowledge gained from the chapter. Here are the first ones.

Learning Points

So what did we learn from this chapter?

Commerciality

Commerciality means thinking like a CEO. Think commercially about everything and don't limit yourself to internal aspects. Analyse how external forces impact key parties in your story and always ask yourself why?

Awareness

Awareness comes in different levels of intensity. We feel comfortable in the low and medium levels, but we have to push through to become High Awareness Individuals.

Five Pillars

There are five pillars to commercial awareness. These are skills and concepts we can focus on developing to become more commercially aware. In short, these are Awareness, Analysis, Framework, Engagement, and Simplification.

Actions

What actions can we take *now* to build on what we learned?

Congrats on the New Job!

Next time you read an interesting story in the news, put yourself as the CEO of a company involved in it. If no company is involved, imagine you are a crucial party in the story. This could be anyone from a consumer to a supplier or a government agency. Having established who you are, start thinking commercially about the story and its implications on you and other parties. Note these down and explain their significance in bullet points.

Reflect, Reflect...Reflect

Think about your current level of awareness. What do you do when you read a news story? How much work do you put in daily to develop your awareness? Note down your current level of awareness and think about what you can do to push through and become a High Awareness Individual.

Thinking about Pillars

Focus on the Pillars of Awareness when considering a story. Identify ways to improve on these (don't worry, the book has a lot of suggestions!)

Chapter 2: The Starting Point

You do not rise to the level of your goals. You fall to the level of your systems. James Clear

Starting is Hard

Starting is always hard. This is especially true of something like commercial awareness. When I first started getting into the habit of staying up to date with the news, I was constantly demotivated.

I had no idea what most of the articles I read were even about. It was complicated, time-consuming, and quite frankly boring. Needless to say, I broke my promise to READ 10 ARTICLES A DAY very soon…

And that is something I hear very often. How can I stay on track? How can I balance staying up to date with news whilst studying or working full time? How do I get back into commercial awareness after months of just studying?

The ambitious strategy mentioned above didn't work for me as it was too easy to let go. So I set out to find methods and techniques that would work for me and allow me to stick to my goals. In this chapter, we'll run through my favourites to ensure you enjoy the journey to becoming more commercially aware.

Commercial Awareness is a skill, and like any other skill, you have to keep working hard to improve it. I hope you will find these ideas useful for your journey! We will build on them in later chapters with our practical skills.

Note: This Chapter may feel like one of those feel-good self-improvement books you find on Amazon. I know some parts may sound a bit ridiculous, but a HUGE part of developing your commercial awareness comes from your mindset towards it. That's way it's worth spending a bit of time to set ourselves up for success.

Embrace the Frustration

As with learning any *new* thing, *learning* how to be commercially aware is frustrating. I try to read ten articles a day; I don't understand 97% of what they are saying, I get frustrated and give up. It's normal. I've done it countless times.

To overcome this, it is essential to see this for what it is. A barrier that you can break through. When you start reading an article and don't understand what a few words mean, your brain will automatically switch off. You'll start thinking about something else.

Maybe you can read this tomorrow instead? Perhaps we can go on Instagram?

That's when *you* have to stop yourself. Push through. Give yourself another 25 minutes of uninterrupted attention and consciously control those thoughts.

When you start thinking that this is too hard. Just say to yourself, "let's give this ten more minutes", or "I'm just starting. It's supposed to be hard", or "I can look up what these words mean. It won't stop me".

One of the concepts I remember struggling with the most was that of *short selling*. I didn't understand it when I first heard about it and decided to never look into it further. It was confusing, and I thought I'd be better off without it.

Then in a month, countless articles came out talking about...you guessed it...Short Selling! I'd start reading one, spot this term, and turn to the next. And there it was again. It was an endless cycle.

At that point, I could either choose to ignore most of the news on my feed or finally push through that barrier.

I'm really glad I looked up the term. A quick search gave me a good idea of what this meant, and guess what, it wasn't that bad!

I then started reading around it I was able to develop my knowledge even further. And finally, all those articles that made no sense before started to get slightly clearer.

I can't say the process was as simple for other concepts that scared me, but it showed me how I allowed my frustration to limit my understanding. That is crucial. Never stop yourself from learning for fear of failing or getting frustrated. Learn to embrace that frustration and grow stronger through it.

This is easier said than done and to achieve this; I would highly recommend making Commercial Awareness a habit and *forgetting motivation*.

Forget Motivation

During University, one of my top searches in September and October was: "Commercial Awareness". Coincidentally, this was the time when I was applying for Training Contracts and was *motivated* to understand what the hell commercial awareness was and what story I could bring to interviews to look smart.

I think that was one of my greatest mistakes. I would only stay up to date with the news when I was motivated by the idea of getting a job. Of course, the application that commercial awareness plays within our careers is undeniable.

From a legal perspective, we get into the whole idea of commercial awareness because we hear the term thrown around at law fairs, events, interviews, assessment centres, etc.

The mistake was not keeping up with the news when I was not applying for jobs. I felt that I had to be *motivated* to open the business section of The Guardian and read the latest stories.

I failed to understand that Motivation is not the spark that gets us to do hard work. It's the **Result**!

As Jeff Haden put it: "Motivation" as we know it is a myth. Motivation isn't the special sauce that we require at the beginning of any significant change. Motivation is a result of the process, not a cause. Understanding this will change the way you approach any obstacle or big goal.

So don't wait for application season to come round or for a magic dose of inspiration. Start tonight. Start tomorrow morning. Just start, regardless of how you feel, because once you get started, you will be *motivated* and proud of what you have accomplished.

This is a marathon, not a sprint, and to succeed, you must also forget about your goals.

No Goals

Commercial Awareness is a skill and not a ticked box. I wanted to emphasise that because we need to forget about the Goal.

Take Jerry Seinfeld as an example. He said that the only way to write better jokes is to write every day. To do this, Seinfeld came up with the "don't break the chain" idea whereby he would draw an X through every day he would write new jokes. The chain of X's will grow, and "your only job is not to break the chain."

There is one caveat with the Seinfeld Method. You must pick a task that makes a difference but can quickly get done. So my plan to read 10 Articles a Day was not sustainable for me. I wasn't able to complete it most days, and it became easier to drop the habit.

Choose actions that are simple to keep on top of and lead you to your desired outcome. To start my commercial awareness *habit*, I decided to set aside 20 minutes every morning to check out the latest news. I would then write a summary of 1 story that caught my eye.

The summary could be as short as a few bullet points, but it gave me a sense of completion and allowed me to start a *chain* that I did not want to break.

At the end of the month, I'd have around 30 story summaries that I could review and link with one another. This made a massive difference to my awareness of trends. I finally figured out that stories do not just occur on their own but are instead built on a larger framework.

Note: This specific task worked for me, but it may not work for you. Maybe you have more time in the evening, or perhaps you want to record your voice instead of writing a summary.

Find a meaningful and straightforward task that works for you and build a chain of it. To ensure you stick to it, you will probably want a solid system in place.

Building Systems

A crucial part of sticking to a habit is building a system that you can focus on.

This is simply a process that will help make it easy for you to become commercially aware. The beauty is you can pick whatever you want because all that matters is that it works for you.

To identify what system works for me, I'd ask myself these questions:

- What time of the day am I usually free?

- What type of format do I prefer to learn from, e.g. audio, written?

- What is a simple yet meaningful amount of time I can spend days developing my Commercial Awareness?

These are straightforward questions, but they should indicate when you can block out time in your daily calendar for your system.

For me, this was as simple as:

- *15 minutes x 2 times a day*

- *Which is 30 mins per working day*

- *Which is 150 minutes a week (2.5hrs)*

- *Which is 10 hours a month.*

This system builds on the 20 min morning routine I mentioned earlier and takes it a step further. This worked even better for me because it allowed me to get a snapshot view of what was coming up in the morning. I then built on it in the evening with a review of what happened and a quick look at what was coming up the next day.

This is a straightforward system and you are free to check out the news beyond these times or read for longer! The main thing is that you maintain your system as your minimum standard and never break the chain. Focus on your process each day, and don't worry about understanding everything or standing out in an interview with an unheard-of story.

Stick to the process, and you will achieve your goals without even realising it.

Avoid Comparison but love discussion

One last point I wanted to highlight is understanding the difference between comparison and discussion. This may seem quite obvious, but I would lie if I did not admit to comparing my achievements or my understanding of commercial awareness to others.

Just like any journey, we travel at our speed. Don't get de-motivated if you go to a law fair and overhear someone impress a senior associate from a London firm with their knowledge of decentralised finance.

If you are sitting with friends discussing the day's news (yes, of course - we love our commercial awareness, don't we??) and your explanation of blockchain gets destroyed by your friend, don't get demotivated.

There will always be someone who will know more about a topic than us. If you find yourself in that situation, enjoy it. Discussion is one of the best things you can rely on to grow more commercially aware.

Walk up to that person and ask them a question about De-Fi. Turn to your friend and ask them for their views on blockchain. Engage in the discussion even when you feel like you know nothing, especially when you think you know everything there is to know.

You will be surprised at how much you can learn from others. This may feel like a random point to make, but one aspect that holds up people when trying to develop their commercial awareness is the fear of looking like we know nothing.

That awkward moment when your friends talk about a topic you have no clue of for 30 minutes is what you should seek. It's not awkward. Don't be demotivated. Admit you may not know much and engage in the discussion. That's 30 mins of learning you get for free!

Travel at your own pace and engage in discussion. You can do this.

Last Thoughts

Don't wait for motivation to come to you. It's a myth. You have to believe in yourself and have the discipline to stick to your habit and systems... You will figure out what process works for you that way. Some may not work, and that is ok. Put them aside and try another one.

Developing your commercial awareness is a long journey, and you need to be in it mentally. The start will be the most challenging part, then day by day, you will grow prouder and more confident in the skills we will touch upon in the following chapters.

Learning Points & Actions

Learning Points

So what did we learn from this chapter?

Frustration & Motivation

As with any new thing, developing your commercial awareness will be frustrating at the start. You need to embrace this frustration and push through this barrier. In the end, you'll love it - you'll see.

And stop waiting for the *motivation* to start. You may feel a bit motivated one day, and it will fade the next. Focus on having the discipline to stick to your habits. Motivation will come as a result as you take pride in what you have achieved.

No Goals, just Systems

Let's not focus on goals. Let's instead focus on our systems. These are processes that make sticking to becoming commercially aware easy. This could be as simple as reading the top business news every morning and writing a summary of your favourite one. The critical thing is that once you get started, you don't stop. You don't break the chain. Focus on the process that works for you, and you will develop your commercial awareness without even realising it.

Actions

What actions can we take *now* to build on what we learned?

Open Up Excel!

Open up Excel or Google Sheets. In the left column, write story, then summary, then Trend. Try to add one story per day or one every two days to this sheet. No need to add tons of information, just enough to remind you what it's about.

In the Sector column, put what specific area the story relates to, e.g. Crypto, Banking, US-UK Trade. You can be as detailed as you want. In the Trend, column bullet points any trends you can think of, e.g. Rise of Crypto, Struggle of Retail, ESG growth, etc. Then review after a month and see how you can collect these stories in different sections and build links between them. You can colour code them to easily spot similar topics or use the classic Ctrl + F to search them.

	A	B	C	D
	Daily News Summary			
1	Story	Summary	Sector	Trend
2				
3				
4				
5				
6				
7				
8				

Example Daily News Summary Spreadsheet

33

Find Your Task

Think about a simple yet meaningful task you can perform daily to develop your commercial awareness. It has to be something that works for you. Then give it a go!

Shrug Off Doubt

Whenever you are reading a news article that you feel is too complicated or open up the news and feel like you can push it to tomorrow/later, ask yourself to give a little more. Don't give up immediately. When you shrug off initial doubt, you will find it easier to persevere and stick to your daily task. You can do this!

Chapter 3: How to Pick the *right* story?

Does choosing the right story matter?

One of the questions we get asked most frequently at TBU is *"What story should I discuss in my interview?"*.

This is something that I always used to wonder about once I started to put some serious effort into becoming commercially aware via the systems we mentioned earlier.

What story will make me stand out in an interview?

This was the question I kept repeating in my head. I had to find the story with a great catchy title, filled with complex jargon and unique trends that would impress the interviewer.

The real question I should have been asking myself was: *"What story would I love to talk about?"* because that is what truly matters. Interviewers see countless candidates, and odds are you will probably bring the same story as someone else.

Interviewers are usually quite experienced, and it's relatively easy for them to see if you know what you are talking about or just skimmed through the BBC News article last night (see me in Preface).

To overcome this put yourself at the centre of the decision-making process. Don't try to guess what the interviewer will be impressed by, take it in your own hands.

Don't feel you have to pick the latest inexplicable update on Brexit food standards just because it sounds clever. If that interests you, go ahead, but if you know that it dœsn't as much as Vegan Food, then why pick it?

You have to find what *you* are interested in.

This will allow you to speak enthusiastically about a subject and subconsciously pick the right story. To do this, just like we did in the last chapter, we want to focus on the process, i.e. figuring out what we love reading about, rather than the goal, i.e. finding the perfect story.

But how do we go about doing this efficiently?

The IPG Method

To pick out the stories that worked best for me, I created the IPG Method. Sound fancy, I know. It stands for Interests, Purpose, and Gaps.

I love using this method because it lets me quickly plot down what I'm looking for and understand what type of story will provide me with the most value.

I'm at the centre of the process and can focus on it rather than the need to find a "good story".

Let's take a look at what each section entails so that you can start using it as soon as possible!

Interests

Remember how we mentioned you need to focus on what you would enjoy discussing? That is what this section of the IPG method involves.

Start by focusing on what you are *interested* in. This will give you a head start and allow you to persevere through the more challenging steps of Analysis we will consider later in the book.

We can see interests as our desire to learn something. They may arise through your natural curiosity, experiences, and goals. For example, I am interested in learning more about **legal tech** because I work in the legal sector and want to understand how this could facilitate legal work in the future.

So I believe interests are undeniably built on past experiences. However, we also pick them based on our present situations to further our goals in the future. Let's take a look at some quick questions you can use to start identifying your interests.

Focus Questions

- What interests and hobbies do you have?

- In the last two months, what stories stood out to you?

- What topic did these stories focus on?

We then need to apply these to a new story to understand if we are interested in it through more specific questions.

Story Selection

- Can you create a link between your interest areas identified above and this story?

- Would this story stimulate your interests?

- Would this story allow you to explore your interests further?

Note: the story doesn't have to be full of interest to you. You will encounter stories that will have only a few elements of interest. However, creating that link between your interests and the story will facilitate your understanding. It will push you to read more into it and make the whole process easier.

Purpose

Now that we identified what you are interested in, we can move on to Step 2 and explore your **Purpose**.

Once more, put yourself at the centre of this process and now focus on what you want to achieve. This could be a short-term goal, e.g. within the next year, or longer-term, e.g. ten years+. You can pick the time frame and the goal.

When I started getting into commercial awareness, my goal was to get a Training Contract. This would then lead me to my current goal of qualifying as a solicitor.

Your purpose can morph through time, but it's always good to have one in focus. To help you get started, you may want to run through these questions.

Focus Questions

- What do you want to achieve? (This could be a career achievement, e.g. a job or a general awareness growth. Your goal is personal to you.)

- What have you stopped yourself from pursuing and doing for fear of failing?

- And my favourite...in 2038, you are giving a TED Talk: What is the topic of your speech?

Story Selection

Having established your interest in the story, it is essential to analyse how a particular story fits your purpose.

- How could this story help you achieve your goal?

- How will this story push me beyond my comfort zone on this topic?

- How will you implement what you learn from this story to reach your goal?

For example, if I am applying for a job at a law firm that specialises in Private Equity in the Technology Sector, I will be keener to pick a story in this field rather than a story discussing marine wildlife.

A well-chosen story can develop your knowledge and confidence. This will allow you to impress your interviewer and explore your interests further.

Gaps

The last point on our model is crucial. The extent to which you address your *gaps* in knowledge is directly proportionate to the rate of growth of your commercial awareness.

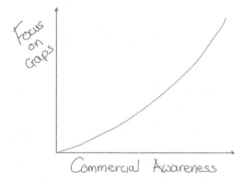

An extremely complex graph showing the degree of proportionality between focus on gaps and commercial awareness development

We grow our understanding the most when we address our weak areas.

If you enjoy reading about the big companies producing batteries for electric cars, you may find it comfortable just to limit yourself to that area.

However, you should take that interest as your starting point and always be on the lookout for areas you know less about. Considering the above example, you may see a lot about what companies are leading the way in the development of batteries, but you may not know as much about the actual process behind them, what they could mean for traditional car producers or what happens to dead batteries?

It's hard, if not impossible, to know every single thing about a topic. This is excellent news for us. It means there are countless possibilities you can explore for whichever case you choose and develop your commercial awareness daily.

You will find that the more you learn, the more gaps you discover. As you start diving deeper and deeper into a topic, you will uncover details you would have never heard about before.

To get you started, here are a few focus questions!

Focus Questions

- What areas of your interests and purpose do you know less about?

- Is there any area you have always chosen to ignore because you felt it was too complicated or boring?

- Have you ever read a term you didn't know the meaning of and chose to ignore it instead of reading about it?

Having examined these let's take a look at some more story-specific questions.

Story Selection

- Are there any areas in this story's topic that you feel slightly weaker on?

- How could this story help you develop your knowledge in these and generally?

- Why will this story make you more commercially aware?

Reflecting on gaps is crucial to identifying how to improve. A story may be of interest and fit your purpose but may be identical to what you already read. Therefore it would not add as much value to you like a story that was of interest and fit your purpose but tackled an area that was *completely new* to you.

So choose the story that scares you. That's the one that will teach you the most.

Last Thoughts

As you start applying the IPG method and progress in your journey to becoming more commercially aware, you will inevitably begin to develop your commercial niche(s).

If you've been staying up to date with the news, you may have noticed gravitating towards a particular topic area. This could be anything from Technology to Politics to more specific topics like Special Purpose Acquisition Companies.

You should try to identify what areas you are most interested in as you become more commercially aware. This feeds perfectly into the IPG method we just ran through.

Indeed, figuring out your Niche(s) will allow you to have a firm grasp of your interests. This will help you identify areas of missing information to select your gaps and elements of further knowledge to stimulate your purpose.

You do not need to focus on just one niche. You can have as many as you want because these are the areas you are interested in. Moreover, if you have a broader selection, you can see how they intersect and strengthen your analytical skills.

The easiest way to build your niche is to avoid cutting off stories based on the title. You may find some articles with extremely complicated or boring titles that just put you off reading them, even if you know they could add some value to your niche.

In these instances, give the story a shot. It may relate to your interests more than you think and potentially allow you to discover things you had no idea existed. (That's a bit profound, but you get what I mean!)

Learning Points & Actions

Learning Points

So what did we learn from this chapter?

Focus on Yourself

The IPG method has been a great way to find the best stories to analyse and discuss. The key to achieving its full potential comes from placing yourself at the centre of the process.

Focus on what *you* are interested in and what you want to achieve to identify the stories that will provide you with the most value.

Choose the Scary Option

If you have a choice between a story covering a topic you have read about before and one that covers a wholly new topic, choose the latter. Don't be intimidated by complicated titles or articles. Give them a go and try to dissect complex terms. The first option may still provide us with some new knowledge but not the same extent as the second one.

You should focus on identifying your Gaps, i.e. areas of missing information within your areas of interest. Once you find these, lean into them and actively search for stories that will fill the gaps and help you develop your knowledge. The speed at which you become more commercially aware is directly proportional to your focus on these gaps. So don't be scared of new concepts and stories. Try them out!

Actions

What actions can we take *now* to build on what we learned?

Find your Goals

Note down your goals on a piece of paper. Don't overthink what you are writing. Just focus on noting down what you would like to achieve (let yourself THINK BIG!)

Pick the one you know nothing about

Next time you see two stories relating to your area of interest. Pick the one you know nothing about. If you see a story on something you never heard of, give it a read. You may discover something you love.

Growing you Niche(s)

On an Excel Sheet, plot down areas you are interested in. These could be anything from Technology to Politics and as specific as Patents. Have a sheet for each and record new stories with titles and summaries that relate to them. After a month, review them and see if you can create any links between the areas in a separate column.

I like to build this into the Daily News Summary Spreadsheet we discussed earlier to create a broader database of stories!

	A	B	C	D
1	Technology			
2	Story	Summary	Trend	Link
3				
4				
5				
6				
7				
8				

Mix it in with the Daily News Summary template for ultimate results!

Chapter 4.1: How to Analyse a Story - Micro-focus

One of the most common queries we receive relates to how to analyse a story.

There are so many different structures ranging from SWOT to PESTLE that get thrown around, and it's pretty hard to know which one is best to use.

In this chapter, we will run through some key analysis tools with some tips and tricks you can use to make the most of them.

The Analysis stage is crucial in our Commercial Awareness journey. Growing more accustomed to it will allow you to deliver discussions in interviews with greater confidence which will, in turn, help you stand out in assessment centres.

We will be running through several different tools for analysis, starting with a focus on our Hypothetical Client and moving on to the broader market.

I tend to plot the points I collect on each of these on an app called Craft, as in the example below (Note: it is only available on iOS, but a great alternative is Notion!).

Fever-Tree Analysis

Micro-Focus on Company

SWOT   Porter's 5 Forces

That way, I can quickly skim through them to tie my analysis together and get ready for the discussion which we will consider in the next chapter.

Learning Example

Before we dive into the various tools, I'll quickly summarise a news story we will be referencing as we progress. Having an example at hand makes these tools less theoretical and helps us see how to adapt each element practically.

So the story we will use is:

Fever-Tree profits take a hit from logistics challenges

By Press Association 2021

Richmond & Twickenham Times article

I could have picked the classic Company A buys Company B for £X, but this one caught my eye as I frankly don't know a lot about Fever-Tree or its industry. So I chose the story that *scares* me and pushes me beyond my comfort zone.

Finding your Hypothetical Client

Picking out your *Hypothetical Client* (**HP**) from stories will allow you to resonate with what the firm is looking for. The HP is the entity at the centre of your story. There may be multiple ones, but it's better if you can pin it down to one.

Our entire analysis in this chapter will revolve around our HP, which in this case is Fever-Tree. We will analyse this story from Fever-Tree's lawyers' perspective to show our interviewer how well we perform in this sort of scenario.

That is what interviewers are looking for: someone that can identify challenges for their clients and come up with innovative legal and commercial solutions. So let's make it super clear to them that we can do this by gearing our analysis around our HP!

Breaking the Terminology Barrier

Picking Out Key Points

The obvious first step in analysing any story is *reading* it. I like to run through a couple of times and highlight key points that can feed into my analysis later on.

I tend to use

- **Yellow** for anything to do with the company that can feed into our SWOT analysis

- **Blue** for Trends that can link to our Trend Tracking

- **Green** for broader market considerations that link to our PESTLE analysis

- **Orange** for Legal considerations for our Legal Focus points

So here are some examples I picked out and summarised:

Yellow: Rising costs of logistics. Slow growth: up 4% to £50.4 million. Strong sales in Europe up 102% helped by the takeover of Global Drinks Partnership (German Distributor). The company was able to overcome driver shortages and manage rising costs.

Blue: Supermarket sales up 17%. Rising costs impacting profit margins across the market. Reopening in the UK on 19 July, seeing larger events restarting and creating opportunities for companies like Fevertree.

Green: Covid related logistics problems. During the past six months, the cost of a container to ship to the US East Coast has increased by 35%, and to the West Coast by 60%. Truck Driver shortage.

Orange: Distribution contracts. Termination clauses. Who is responsible for failure to deliver? Can costs be increased if agreed in a contract?

Start Small

The best way to approach a story involving a company is to start small and expand as we progress.

This will allow us to identify critical elements at a Micro level i.e. for the business, before moving on to the Macroelements involving global trends and the economy as a whole.

If you are interviewing for a law firm or any client-focused business, this is a great way to showcase your understanding of the client's goals, needs, and concerns. This will ultimately make you a more attractive candidate and help you stand out from the competition.

SWOT

SWOT is a brilliant process to use to start this micro analysis section as it allows you to quickly identify critical aspects of the entity involved. It involves background research on your side, which forces us to take an analytical view of the story rather than a merely descriptive one.

Let's look at what each section entails and how you can make the most of them.

S: Strengths

Look at how the company distinguishes itself from its competitors and its Unique Selling Point(s) (**USP**). This can be in terms of branding, technology, and services (to name a few).

It's easy to fall into the idea that any "good" thing a company has going for it is a strength. We should still consider these, but predominantly focus on aspects that give a company a *clear* competitive advantage.

These are aspects which the company has and very few/none of its competitors can claim. Think of elements that are visible and make the company stand out when compared to its rivals.

Let's try to apply this to our Fever-Tree example.

Example: A few key strengths of Fever-Tree are Clear Marketing and Product Focus. The company was able to capture the market of premium mixers to complement the premium alcoholic drinks. They target this market area with powerful advertising to make themselves the go-to brand for quality mixers. Gin sales grew by 56% between 2011 and 2017 in the UK, and Fever-Tree was able to ride this wave to overtake Schweppes.

The Company's focus to deliver High-End Mixers is very clear. Most people will know what Fever-Tree is and/or does even without purchasing their products. They know what their clients want and make it very clear that they are the brand they want.

In my analysis, I also considered strong distribution chains and successful expansion strategy as some relevant points. However, branding and product focus are crucial USPs and, in my opinion, are what makes Fever-Tree stand out in the market. When selecting your points, be sure to highlight:

- Why are they Unique Selling Points?

- What actual and/or potential effect have they had on the company?

W: Weaknesses

Weaknesses are a crucial part of our SWOT analysis because they allow us to showcase our problem-solving skills. This section should focus on identifying areas where the company can improve to match or even surpass its competitors.

If you are applying to be a lawyer or any service-focused role, this is a brilliant opportunity for you to show to your interviewer your potential value to clients. Quite often, clients come to lawyers with problems they need to be solved. As a lawyer, you would consider not only the legal aspects of the issue but also its commercial points.

Identifying what your client's weaknesses are is a massive part of advising on the best course of action to take. That is why we want to clarify to our interviewer that we know how to do this.

Using a real company to showcase shows the interviewer we can adapt our problem-solving skills to real-world scenarios. We do not stop at the theoretical level.

So in this section, let's focus on identifying the weaknesses to set ourselves up to offer excellent solutions.

Example:

We will base this section on the points we highlighted in yellow whilst reading the story.

- What weaknesses does the company possess? This can include elements such as what their competitors are doing better than them, unclear USP, and things they can improve on.

- What does company Y have that company X doesn't?

Some considerations for Fevertree could be:

- Limited success outside its core gin mixer business. You could argue whether this is a true weakness as it helps with branding but usually having only one key product/service can be a risky play.

- Marketing of products should be improved to make the product stand out even more and fight off growing competition in the market. Heavy reliance on word of mouth can be limiting.

- Organisational structure is heavily reliant on the current business model and complicates move to other ones

- Young brand - will need to invest in marketing to build consumer trust and brand recognition further compared to some of its bigger rivals e.g. Schweppes

O: Opportunities

If Strengths are what sets the company apart at present, **Opportunities** are what can make it stand out in the future.

To successfully tackle this section, we need to look at opportunities the company may exploit when attempting to improve its positioning in the market(s) it operates in.

This part requires a degree of knowledge of the market you're discussing and an ability to make informed predictions.

Whereas in the Strengths and Weaknesses sections we were focusing more heavily on the company's profile, in this part of our analysis we will look at the *Broader picture.*

We want to consider what other companies in the market are doing, what our company is missing out on at present, what trends we are seeing in consumer habits etc.

Try to put yourself in the shœs of the company's CEO. Opportunities can be based on stuff your company is doing now, but in some cases, top opportunities come from things your company is not doing yet.

Abercrombie & Fitch started as a fishing gear store and became a top clothing brand. Netflix used to send movies to customers by post before seeing and taking the *opportunity* for online content to become the king of streaming. Nokia started as a paper manufacturer in Nokia, Finland, before moving into electronics and telecommunications.

There are endless examples, and especially nowadays, companies must be able to adapt rapidly to market demands to succeed. That is what we are looking for in this section. The ideas that could help our company outperform the market.

Example

For this section, we can look at the elements we highlighted in green and yellow as this will allow us to assess the market as a whole and pick out critical opportunities for Fevertree.

Some opportunities for Fevertree could be:

- Being ready to match the growing demand for gin

- Partnerships with smaller craft gin producers to stand out from the competition and match the growing demand for small distillers

- Focus on becoming a leader in *healthy* mixers to become the mixer of choice for younger consumers who tend to look for healthier product options.

- Focus on online sales as more people grow accustomed to purchasing products online.

- Subscription business to deliver gin mixer directly to consumers and ensure recurring cash flow.

- A consumer referral program for online sales to boost brand recognition, consumer trust, and overall sales.

- Partnerships with major hotel chains to become the mixer of choice and develop a high-quality brand image.

T: Threats

Keeping an eye out for **Threats** is just as important as looking closely at Opportunities.

Major companies have been put out of business because they did not see Threats coming.

In the late 90s, Blockbuster had over 9,000 video-rental stores in the US, 84,000 employees worldwide, and 65 million registered customers.

Ten years later, Blockbuster filed for bankruptcy with over $900 million in debt.

What happened? Simple, Blockbuster saw the Threat of Streaming and Netflix coming but did little about it.

It even turned down a $50 million deal to buy Netflix, which was worth 194 billion in 2020. Blockbuster failed to innovate on streaming and to match its competition, eliminated late fees, which were a crucial part of its revenue stream.

Identifying threats early is one of the best ways for a company to avoid weaknesses. If a company can tackle these effectively, it can prevent losing market shares, customers, profits, etc. Showing you can see these threats for what they are is a fantastic way to stand out in interviews.

With regards to the Competition Threat, we want to look at various types of competitors. These can be categorised under five main categories, namely:

- Direct

- Potential

- Indirect

- Future

- Replacement

Look at anything that may pose a threat to the company and negatively affect its growth. It may not be obvious. Blockbuster didn't see Netflix as a major threat otherwise it would have bought it for $50 million. The sooner you find them and act on them, the better the company will manage their impact.

Example

Competition is undoubtedly a key threat for Fevertree. With a growing number of choices in the market, the company may be subject to the risk of product substitution in the consumer's eyes who may choose to pick a cheaper, new, or simply different alternative.

The food and drinks industry is highly regulated, and this could pose threats to its products should they come under scrutiny. This may lead to costs involved in litigation or reinstatement of reputation after losses to its brand credibility.

Fevertree took a leading position in the market by being *early* but has since been following other big players' moves. The products it introduced are more *responsive* than innovative, and this could present a threat to its position if competitors were able to innovate more and leave the company behind.

Porter's Five Forces (PFF)

Another classic tool in the commercial world is Porter's Five Forces. You may have heard of this a few times and wondered what they are or whether they are even relevant (I know I did).

So let's have a run through them as they will prove very useful for our analysis and discussion to help us get an edge in interviews.

What are these 5 Forces?

Porter's Five Forces were ideated by...you guessed it, Mr Porter (Michael Porter). He said these five forces have crucial impacts on a company's profitability in the market.

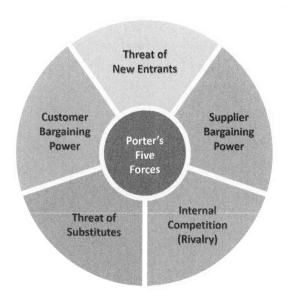

These are:

- Threat of New Entrants

- Bargaining Power of Suppliers

- Bargaining Power of Buyers

- Threat from Substitute Products

- Rivalry among the existing players

In short, the success and profitability of our selected company is based on the strength of these forces. The weaker the forces, the greater the opportunity for better performance. On the other hand, the stronger the forces, the greater the challenge to take home high returns.

This is an essential part of our analysis because it helps us understand the challenges faced by our target company. This allows us to assess the best strategy to find a position in the market that it can defend from competition to ultimately thrive.

This is a fantastic tool to showcase in an interview scenario. It proves to the interviewer that you are able to analyse the past and present situation and offer astute strategies that will help your selected company succeed.

If you are interviewing for a role in the legal sector, this is a massive green tick for the interviewer. As a lawyer, you must be able to advise not only on the legal aspects of a matter but crucially also on the commercial implications it raises. The same applies to most roles in the services industry where you assist clients with personal and professional matters.

Law firms want people that can offer reasonable and innovative solutions to their client problems. Using PFF will let you find the issues and lead you to these solutions.

So that's all great stuff - but how do we apply PFF? Let's take a look at Fevertree!

Threat of New Entrants

As Porter put it: "New entrants to an industry bring new capacity, the desire to gain market share, and often substantial resources".

A great resource to get us started and find suggested competitors for most well-known companies is Craft.co. All you have to do is plug in your company in the search bar and select their profile.

From there you can select the competitors tab and see at a glance their top competitors. We also get some useful data insights ranging from their founding date and company type to their revenue and cost of goods. You should be able to check this for free.

Fever-Tree competitors

Clear all

Fever-Tree's top competitors include Fentimans, Thomas Henry, The Coca-Cola Company and Brewers Supply Group.

Q Add company...

Fever-Tree ⊗   Fentimans ⊗   Thomas Henry ⊗   The Coca-Cola Co... ⊗   Brewers Supply G... ⊗

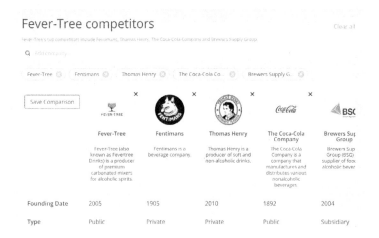

	Fever-Tree	Fentimans	Thomas Henry	The Coca-Cola Company	Brewers Sup Group
Save Comparison	Fever-Tree (also known as Fevertree Drinks) is a producer of premium carbonated mixers for alcoholic spirits.	Fentimans is a beverage company.	Thomas Henry is a producer of soft and non-alcoholic drinks.	The Coca-Cola Company is a company that manufactures and distributes various nonalcoholic beverages.	Brewers Sup Group (BSG) supplier of fooc alcoholic bever
Founding Date	2005	1905	2010	1892	2004
Type	Public	Private	Private	Public	Subsidiary

For Fever-Tree, a new entrant threat could be Thomas Henry. Founded in 2010 in Berlin, Germany it focuses on a very similar market to Fever-Tree.

Having identified the potential threat we want to show our interviewer how Fever-Tree can protect itself from it. To do this, you should refer to barriers to entry to the market. There are six major barriers, namely:

1. **Economies of scale:** when more units of a good or service can be produced on a larger scale with fewer costs. This forces new entrants to come in big or accept a cost disadvantage.

2. **Product differentiation:** Brand Identification leading to customer loyalty

3. **Capital requirements:** Need to invest large sums to compete

4. **Cost disadvantages independent of size:** technology, experience, subsidies, favourable locations, etc.

5. **Access to distribution channels:** how tied up distribution channels are to existing competitors

6. **Government policy:** regulations and laws

The crux of it is that the higher the barriers to entry, the harder it is for new entrants to break through and take a share of the market.

In the food and drink industry, some obvious high barriers to entry would be access to distribution channels, product differentiation, and capital requirements.

Breaking through this industry takes a lot of money and time to establish solid distribution agreements that would allow new entrants to outperform current market holders.

Moreover, Fever-Tree has a strong and identifiable brand that generates customer loyalty. Thomas Henry would need to invest sizable amounts of money to overcome this.

The best strategy here is to go through those six barriers and think how does this relate to my story and company? Some will not apply every time so it is important to pick out the most applicable ones and explain why so that your interviewer sees your ability to prioritise solutions.

Bargaining Power of Suppliers & Buyers

Suppliers can exert bargaining power on participants in an industry by raising prices or reducing the quality of purchased goods and services.

By raising their prices, soft drink concentrate producers have contributed to the erosion of profitability of bottling companies because the bottlers, facing intense competition from powdered mixes, fruit drinks, and other beverages, have limited freedom to raise their prices accordingly.

When considering this aspect we need to examine what suppliers our selected company will have to rely on. A company like Fever-Tree will rely on flavour concentrate producers and bottlers to make its products.

The extent of the impact these suppliers can have will be dependant on:

- the uniqueness of the product they are supplying

- the number of companies dominating the industry and;

- the importance of our company as a customer to them.

Similarly, customers can force down prices, demand higher quality or more service, and play competitors off against each other—all at the expense of industry profits.

When considering how powerful a buyer group is, try to determine if:

- It is concentrated or purchases in large volumes

- It earns low profits, which creates a great incentive to lower its purchasing costs. Highly profitable buyers tend to be less cost-sensitive.

- Can it save customers money? (Pay for itself many times over - e.g. accounting or accurate surveys of properties)

- Can they easily find an alternative product?

Porter suggests that, as a rule, a company can sell to powerful buyers and still come away with above-average profitability only if it is a low-cost producer in its industry or if its product enjoys some unusual, if not unique, features.

In an interview, you want to show that you clearly understand how suppliers and buyers interact with your chosen company. This will prove your commercial understanding of how costs and profitability are impacted by external parties and allow you to offer valuable strategic solutions for your hypothetical client.

Threat from Substitute Products

Substitutes limit an industry's potential returns by placing a ceiling on the prices that firms within that industry can charge to make a profit. As the price-performance alternative offered by substitutes becomes more attractive, it becomes even more difficult for those firms to make a profit.

If Thomas Henry broke into the market with a gin mixer priced at 59p, it would probably attract a good amount of Fever-Tree's customers who would rather save up on this than pay £1.80 for a Fever-Tree mixer. (Unless they are very loyal customers - of course!)

Having such a cheap substitute on the market is problematic for Fever-Tree as it places a ceiling on the price they can charge for their products. They know that as it stands they would struggle to attract customers and they will be more inclined to decrease their prices to compete.

This could harm their profit margins and may prove even more costly if their suppliers demand higher payments.

Identifying substitutes involves searching for other products or services that can perform the same function as the industry's product or service.

Substitute products that deserve the most attention strategically are those that

1. are subject to trends improving their price-performance tradeoff with the industry's product, or

2. are produced by industries earning high profits.

Highlighting how a given product or company could be taken out by a substitute is fundamental to showing your understanding of competition. It will help you determine strategies and anticipate threats for your selected company.

Rivalry among the existing players

A key part of the market is determined by existing players. We must look at the way they interact with each other to determine how our company can step up and succeed in the long term.

When assessing whether an industry has a high level of rivalry, consider:

72

- How many competitors are there and are they equal in size?

- Is Industry growth slow? This prevents expanding market shares.

- Are Exit Barriers high?

In selecting a story focused on a company, try to look at its current competitors and identify their strategies. If you were the CEO of this company, what would you be worried about? How would you counter these challenges?

Some common solutions you can mention are for the company to focus on the fastest-growing areas of the market or areas with lower fixed costs. Fever-Tree could ride the rise in popularity of healthy drinks or increase its production of lemon flavoured drinks (if these were less costly to produce).

Competition is inevitable since no business operates alone in a vacuum. Despite its negative connotations, competition can also be a factor in pushing companies to develop better products and become industry leaders.

The key here is to show your interviewer that you can identify the current competition and take the initiative to suggest ways for our hypothetical client to surpass them.

Showing Your Strategy to the Interviewer

Once you've run through these different areas of competition, you will need to plot them down in your analysis to formulate a strategy that you can show your interviewer. To do this, focus on these three key points:

- What strengths and areas should the company focus on to best protect itself from the competition?

- What moves would allow it to improve its current market position?

- How can it anticipate upcoming threats and which new strategies should it pursue to counter them?

If you run through these questions you will be able to note down an effective strategy for the company. No one is expecting you to solve all their problems and bring them to the top of the S&P 500. Just provide some realistic and innovative solutions that address their challenges to help them strive and explain *WHY* you think so.

Moving On

Now that we have analysed the company at the centre of our selected story we can move on to the broader picture. This will show our interviewer that we have a deep level of commercial awareness as we can link a story we picked to major trends in the global markets! (That sounds good dœsn't it??)

Remember that in some stories, you will have more than one company to consider e.g. if you select a story regarding a merger. That is fine! Run through this analysis on both and think analytically as a lawyer what point you would raise if you were advising them.

Before we move on, let's have a quick check of our Learning Points and Actions!

Learning Points

So what did we learn from this chapter?

Highlight Time

Use a colour scheme to highlight key points from an article so that you can easily slot them into your analysis tools. I tend to use:

- **Yellow** for anything to do with the company that can feed into our SWOT analysis

- **Blue** for Trends that can link to our Trend Tracking

- **Green** for broader market considerations that link to our PESTLE analysis

- **Orange** for Legal considerations for our Legal Focus point (This is still useful to know even if you're not applying to work in the legal industry!)

SWOT

When analysing your hypothetical client at the centre of your story start with SWOT. This is a great way for us to identify what our HP is doing well and what it could expand on by tackling its threats and weaknesses. It will show your interviewer that you can critically analyse your HP.

This is a great skill to showcase because it shows you have what it takes to be a lawyer and advise clients effectively on what they need.

PFF

PFF ties in well with our SWOT analysis. It takes our analysis of HP's threats a step further by categorising each one in the 5 different threats sections.

Combining this with our SWOT analysis allows us to show our interviewer not only that we can identify problems but also anticipate challenges that lie further ahead.

The idea here is that preventing something is better than curing it. If you can show that you can spot something that has not hit our HP yet and explain why it could become a problem, you'll stand out in interviews!

Action Points

What actions can we take *now* to build on what we learnt?

Write It Down

Pick a Story from the News. Then take your favourite note-taking app, journal, or piece of paper and run through it with a SWOT analysis and PFF.

Have a page for SWOT with headings Strengths, Weaknesses, Opportunities, and Threats and another page with the PFF Headings.

No need to go in-depth. Bullet points are fine. Write whatever comes to mind!

Now let's see how to broaden the scope of our analysis!

Chapter 4.2: How to Analyse a Story - The Broader Picture

The Bigger Picture

Now that we have completed a solid analysis of our Hypothetical Client (HP) we want to look around and broaden our view. This is something we touched on when looking at Threats and Opportunities.

The key idea is to focus on *external* factors that could affect our HP's business and strategy. So let's start by looking at the familiar PESTLE analysis before we move on to focus on the **Legal Link** we can identify in our interview!

PESTLE PARTY!

It wouldn't be a proper analysis if we didn't throw in a bit of PESTLE would it?

Alongside SWOT, PESTLE is probably one of the most well-known tools to analyse a news story.

Due to this, we often get asked which one is better? Which one should I use? The answer is simple, use both. These two tools are great because they complement each other. There may be some overlap but they ensure you cover any points you might miss if you focused on only one of them.

So…starting from the basics, **PESTLE** stands for

- Political

- Economic

- Social

- Technological

- Legal

- Environmental

The great thing about PESTLE is that it forces us to think *strategically* just like a real business would. It helps us see what our HP would focus on to develop new products, services, or solutions and anticipate challenges.

It also gives our answers a fuller dimension by placing the story we chose in a wider context.

This means we are not just focusing on why Fever-Tree's sales are down but we are linking it to the impacts that Biden's administration could have on the Drink Mixers market.

Before we get into it, remember Craft, that app we mentioned earlier? It comes in handy here with some more sections for us to add our information in to skim through later! (We are not sponsored by Craft - it just looks pretty and makes notes look nice)

Let's take a closer look at what this means in practice.

Political

When we look at Political aspects, we want to focus on what the governments in the countries our HP is operating in can do.

This is important because their policies and decisions will directly affect what are HP can or cannot do. For example, the UK government imposes a ban on gin mixers that surpass a certain sugar level threshold.

Fever-Tree would have to quickly check it aligns with this. If it does, then no problem but if not that could be a huge problem. It would be unable to sell in the UK and would potentially incur large losses.

From a quick search on Google, here is something we could refer to about Fever-Tree. This page also offers a quick checklist to confirm whether products come under the Levy..that could be an interesting point to mention in an interview to show our interviewer we went a step further by applying it to our HP!

Guidance
Check if your drink is liable for the Soft Drinks Industry Levy

Find out which drinks are liable for the Soft Drinks Industry Levy, and how much you may need to pay.

By the way, the Government website is a great resource to find this sort of information!

Keeping a close eye on what is happening in the politics of a given country is a brilliant asset for you to show in an interview to outline your *full circle* understanding of commercial awareness.

Here is a list of questions that can assist in pinning down any issues:

- What are the country's labour, foreign trade, and governmental policies and how will these impact businesses?

- How will the result of a political election impact investor sentiment?

- Will geopolitical tensions give rise to tariffs? If so, how will this impact imports and exports? Will companies need to move to alternative jurisdictions?

- How will protectionism impact global trade?

- How will the currency react to a 'market-friendly candidate winning an election?

- How will political stability impact markets?

Economical

Well, this is probably the biggest section when thinking about **Commercial** Awareness.

The factors that determine how well the global economy is doing or more specifically the one our HP operates in are crucial to our analysis. (And they score you some nice Commercial Awareness points in an interview)

At the time of writing this, there is a lot of talk around inflation being on the rise. This is a concern for countries worldwide. You don't want inflation to go too high because, put simply, people's purchasing power will drop.

This is something we could easily link to Fever-Tree as they will have to keep an eye on inflation to ensure they are adequately pricing their products. Moreover, if they wanted to take out a loan to expand their operations they would want to check the interest rates to confirm they can afford it.

Bonus Tip: Try to mention how these economic factors impact not only our HP but also the law firm you are applying to. Law Firms are businesses and they will be affected by the economic forces at play.

Identifying these and outlining potential solutions will make you a very interesting candidate for the firm. (No one is asking you to solve inflation - just suggest a few ideas on what central banks could do to keep it in check. A great place to start on this is Investopedia).

Here is a list of questions that can assist in finding these issues (For each one consider how you can apply this to the HP and relate it to the the firm):

- What are the markets like?

- How is the rate of inflation?

- Do consumers have lots of disposable income? Are they spending it or saving it due to negative future forecasting? How will this impact central bank policies?

- What is the unemployment rate like?

- Has the government been using quantitative easing?

Social

This is the section I used to struggle the most with because it requires a bit more analysis into the lifestyle and habits of the people interacting with our HP.

That takes a bit of research but you can figure this out without going into extreme detail.

Do not think you need to precisely pick out the habits of Fever-Tree's customers. Fever-Tree operates in the UK, US, and Spain. So we want to look at the consumer habits in these regions.

A great way to find these is by searching for research or white papers on Google that relates to your HP's market. For Fever-Tree I searched consumer habits in the drinks market and found a website that referenced the Paper pictured above.

From there we can quickly identify how consumers in this market are shifting to healthier drinks as they become increasingly conscious of the ingredients used to produce them. Research Papers like these are usually backed up by statistics which are fantastic for making your points sound well researched.

So instead of saying there is a growing demand for healthy drinks, you could say: Research Paper published by Kerry highlighted that 76% of consumers focus on finding drinks with natural ingredients due to a growing concern of the health implications of artificial products.

Then move on to linking it to your HP. Fever-Tree seems to have picked up on this point...

But don't limit it to just the consumer. Looking at what our HP is doing is also very important and that could be as easy as checking their Corporate Social Responsibility (CSR) strategy on their website!

Here are a few questions that can assist in finding useful points to mention:

- Is a company renowned for its commitment to CSR?

- What are the lifestyle trends among consumers and how are these impacting companies and markets?

- Is the company aiming to become carbon neutral?

- Does a company's commitment to transparent supply chains impact consumer confidence and brand reputation?

- What are your HP's customer's beliefs or buying habits?

Technological

Technology is everywhere and businesses worldwide use it one way or another. You'll find his section easier for some HP's than others. If our HP's operated in the tech or gaming space we could draw more points than we could for Fever-Tree.

Regardless, you want to be open-minded as to the meaning of technology. I used to limit my understanding of this section to tech gadgets e.g. a new phone or computer software. Truth is, technology goes way beyond that and can be identified in the way a company distributes or even creates physical products.

For example, Fever-Tree launched a new line of low-calorie drinks and promoted them during lockdown with digital experiences.

When I read that, I instantly thought of the growing use that businesses are finding for technology like Augmented Reality or VR.

Now it may be a bit out of the box, but what if Fever-Tree could harness these technologies to create experiences for customers. For example, enjoy an evening in Nassau with a Premium Indian Tonic Water Gin.

The customer visits a Fever-Tree VR centre where they can acquire a daily pass to get 5 drinks and the opportunity to enter a VR set feeling in Nassau even if they are in London.

I know…it sounds a bit extravagant but that is what you want to do. Think outside the box and remember to identify what technology is on the rise and link into your HP. You will also gain some extra points if you can then outline how the firm's

IP, corporate and commercial departments could assist to make this a reality.

See it as a time to identify opportunities for your client. Offering ideas that sound a bit crazy but are backed up by reasonable research into technology trends and consumer habit could be what makes you stick in the interviewer's mind as someone that is not afraid to come up with unique ideas.

Here are some quick-fire questions for you:

- Is the company known for innovation? How much money and R&D do they invest in tech and innovation?

- Does the company meet the rapidly changing client and market demands involving tech solutions?

- What is the future of big tech firms?

Legal

I'm going to leave this short and sweet as we'll cover the Legal Points in more depth in the upcoming section. (We love a bit of legal analysis so why not give it its spotlight!)

Here are some quick questions to get you ready for it:

- Does the company have any current, pending, or future litigation?

- Does the business require cross-border collaboration on a multi-jurisdictional matter?

- Is there a specific legal principle or clause that the client should be aware of?

- What is the jurisdiction's antitrust, consumer protection, health and safety, and copyright laws like?

Environmental

This is an extremely important section. It is fundamental for businesses to focus on the environment and how to limit their impact on it.

Firstly, we want to focus on the external factors. These are the effects that natural disasters and climate change could have on our HP.

As Fever-Tree produces drinks, they will be reliant on natural ingredients' availability. This could be affected by floods, fires and other forms of natural events.

As an example, the company's tonic was flavoured with quinine, a chemical extracted from the bark of the South

American cinchona tree. A predominant location for this Tree is Peru.

We can now focus our analysis on this geographical location. From a quick search on Google, we can see that Andean glaciers, of which about 70% are in Peru, are among the fastest retreating mountain ice caps and one of the most visible impacts of the climate crisis. Their retreat can cause huge floods in the country.

The cinchona tree does not solely appear in Peru but a severe event like a flood could greatly harm its supply and in turn harm Fever-Tree's production.

Secondly, we should look at what our HP is doing for the environment, if anything. Fever-Tree has specific sections on its website for this that offer useful points to mention when explaining how climate change affects them. (**Tip:** A simple search of HP Name + Climate Change can bring up useful results!)

CLIMATE

Climate change is a crisis that requires everyone to play their part. As a global business, we recognise the role we have in contributing to the fight, not just in the future but also now. To do so, we have been working with experts to understand and measure our overall climate impact. Being able to understand and measure our impact means we are then able to challenge ourselves and our partners to mitigate and reduce the carbon footprint of our drinks.

Here are some useful questions for you:

- Is the company committed to sustainability or does it form part of a PR move?

- How is sustainability represented in its work practices? Is the company paper free and relies on technology to perform its duties? Does the company implement a cycle to work scheme?

- Is the company engaging in environmentally friendly practices?

- How will natural disasters impact supply and demand?

Trend Tracking

I love Trends.

Why you may ask? Easy - they make us sound clever in an interview.

One of the most common mistakes in analysing and discussing a story in an interview is failing to move from a descriptive to an analytical discussion.

Put simply:

- Descriptive = X happened because of Y.

- Analytical = X happened because Z impacted the markets in W that fed into the growing trends in P that affected Y. (Oversimplified but you get the gist)

Trends force us to move into that analytical phase of our discussion which we will consider in the next chapter. They prompt us to think of the story as a piece of a much broader puzzle rather than on its own.

Remember the trend section in our story tracking template? Well, it comes in handy now as the Trend Tracking phase is a direct step up from it.

Put in a short formula, what we are looking for here is:

History of the News Story + Matching Stories + Look to the Future

So let's open up a new page in our note-taking app or journal and write Trend Tracking for X Story at the top. Under it we will include 1-3 Trends, there is no reason to list dozens of trends. It's best to include less detailed and sensible points than spread yourself thin.

We use our story's market sector as the starting point. As an example, for Fever-Tree this would be the Soft Drinks and Alcoholic Drinks sectors.

Now we can follow the quick 3 Step Formula mentioned above to easily identify our trends.

1. History

Some news providers, like FT, include a short tag of companies at the top of their stories. By clicking it we are led to a page that collects all the stories our HP was mentioned in. This is a useful trick to quickly find past stories and identify any trends.

When I did this for Fever-Tree, I found that the company's sales have been dropping for years with reports in January of 25% drops in sales. This is a very interesting point because it extends our Trend of struggle. Initially, I would have attributed Fever-Tree's struggle to the pandemic but with a quick History Search, we can confidently say that this has been building up for a longer period.

To show that, we could mention how in 2019 it reported an overall growth rate of 10 per cent for the year, which was well below the 40 per cent it reported in 2018.

So Trend Number 1 found! Fever-Tree's Sales Struggles

2. Matching Stories

Time for our second step! We can find matching stories in the article itself in the form of links or the sidebar of the article. If nothing interesting appears here, you can go on to search on your news provider with keywords from your story.

In this case, something like drinks sales logistics challenge/issues could work well. From there you can read a few articles that sound relevant. I tend to read/skim 5-10 articles to find a matching story trend but you may find all you need in 2 or 3!

Some examples I found for our story were in stories showcasing how Nestlé, Procter & Gamble and Unilever all recently set out plans for price rises following **commodity price jumps** and a **spike in logistics costs**.

According to these matching stories, these increases have already led to **rising inflation** in the UK and the US.

So there we have it, a few more trends to add to our list!

3. Look to the Future

The third step of our Trend Analysis can appear to be a bit tricky. We want to find coverage of what our HP is looking to do in the future. This could include strategies, new projects, different products and more.

Anything that gives us an insight into the direction they will be taking and why.

For Fever-Tree, I found that they would resist big price increases to their products. This is a particularly interesting insight because it links up with the price increase plans we noticed in stories about Nestle, Procter & Gamble and Unilever and offers an opposing strategy.

This allows us to reinforce the troubling trend of rising costs for Fever-Tree and match it with the solutions other parties in the market are pursuing.

We can then build on that to show our HP's strategy to outline our holistic understanding of the trends shaping the market our HP operates in.

Trend Roundup

So to summarise the trends we identified are:

1. Fever-Tree's Sales Struggles

2. Inflation

3. Price rises plans

I tend to note these down on a separate sheet and add bullet points under them whenever I find something I think is relevant. That way you can go back to it and quickly identify the main points to mention before your interview.

This is a great exercise to practice your analytical skills beyond the interview preparation stage. It will be useful when we take a look at how to approach case study questions in assessment centres in our next chapter!

The Legal Link

Assuming you are interviewing with a legal firm, it is important to not only know the implications of the story on the stakeholders and the industry but also to know the scope of work arising out of the story.

This will show your interviewer that you understand the work they do and can explain why. This is extremely important because it proves your interest in working for the law firm and allows you to stand out from other candidates who only consider news stories from a strictly commercial perspective.

So how do we do this? Well, an easy way to get started is our 3 Step Legal Link strategy.

1. Research

Start by researching the various practice areas in general. You might already have an idea of many of them if not, no worry! A great place to find these is directly from the website of the law firm you are applying to. Just click on Services or Sectors and they will all be listed there.

This is a great way to find out what sort of work the firm does and pick out points from your story that will match their expertise. This will be crucial in showing them why you want to train *there* instead of at firm X, Y or Z.

Once you have your practice areas, copy them onto a new sheet. This can be in a word doc format with headings or a table format in excel, whatever works best for you!

Going in-depth during your practice sessions will also help you understand the roles of lawyers and the tasks they most commonly take on.

2. Identify

With our table in place let's move on to the next step! We want to go back to a news story and spot the possible areas that would entail legal work.

This will require some analytical thinking from your side. The best way to do this is to think like a lawyer for our HP.

What problems can you identify at present or for the future? Are there any contracts or agreements involved? Where could claims against your HP come from?

Think problems and find the department that is best placed to find a solution.

3. Link

Once you have a few points, you can link them up with the different practice areas and mention why they would be involved.

To do this effectively try to look for similar tasks that lawyers would be expected to take on. You can then try to match these with the examples that law firms usually give under the practice area pages on their websites.

Remember we want to focus on the practice areas the firm we are applying to is particularly strong in or areas they are looking to strengthen for the future. This will show we are keen on joining them and are not just copy-pasting our answers.

To put this in practice, here is an example table for the Fever-Tree story. In this case, we would be applying to a firm with particular expertise in Shipping, Commercial and Banking.

Legal Link

Logistics

Firm Work: supply chain and warehousing agreements, outsourcing contracts, and partnerships and collaborations.

Story Link: Rising logistics costs due to demand rising as pandemic restrictions ease.

Legal Work: Logistics agreements/contracts. Drafting and sticking to them during challenging time. How to protect our client's interest. How to re-negotiatiate contracts or agreements. Insurance to protect client's position.

Commercial

Firm Work: Focus on Supply Chain management. Supply arrangements for goods or services. Standard terms and conditions for best legal position to manage risk.

Story Link: Rising costs lead to reconsidering of supplier and logistics contracts.

Legal Work: Supplier contracts weighing in on decreasing sales. How to draft contracts that safeguard our client's position and do not expose them to too much risk. Re-negotiate contracts.

Banking and Finance

Firm Work: Corporate lending and security, leveraged and acquisition finance, asset based lending and asset finance.

Story Link: Rising costs, decreasing sales and challenges from pandemic may lead Fever-Tree to require loans to pursue growth or offset these challenges.

Legal Work: How to request financing? Facility Agreements, Loans etc. How would a firm advise Fever-Tree on this? To secure documents for theTerm loan facility. Drafting loan agreement. Liaising between the creditors and the company. Negotiating for the credit

Brief Example of Legal Link Analysis. You should go in more depth particularly on the Legal Link section but this should give you an idea!

Learning Points

So what did we learn from this chapter?

Focus on the bigger picture

Don't feel like you need to pick SWOT or PESTLE...use them both and build your analysis at both a small and broader level.

Once you've run through these, focus on Trends. They are a great way to easily bring your analysis to the next level and show that we know what we are talking about. That way you can identify their concerns and come up with unique solutions.

A lawyer must be able to see what is happening in the market at present and what trends will arise in future. By using our Trend Tracking formula you will be able to identify these and exploit them to stand out in your interview.

Legal Link

If you are reading this book, odds are you are applying for a training contract. Therefore, you must mention how your story links to the work the firm you are applying to does.

By using our simple 3 step strategy you can quickly identify points from your story that give rise to work for specific practice areas.

Remember to focus on areas the firm you are applying to is particularly strong in or those in which it is looking to expand its presence in the future.

Action Points

What can we do now to improve?

PESTLE

Remember that story you picked out in the previous chapter? Pick it back out and open your notes. Your first page will focus on PESTLE analysis.

Read the story and 3-5 related stories. Then write down in bullet point format key points you found under each heading. Don't worry about them being perfect. Just start writing what comes to mind. The more you write, the easier it gets!

Legal Link

Every time you research a firm, note down their top practice areas as in the example above. When reading your story or any new story try thinking about what work lawyers would be expected to do and note it down.

If you pick any of these stories for an interview add them to your practice areas notes and follow our example to identify what work you would expect these lawyers to do.

Keep it focused. Some firms will have many practice areas they will be experts in but a few of them will be their absolute top. Focus on these and try to find areas they have been expanding in by sorting through the news...(The Legal Update is a great place to start on that!).

Chapter 5: How to Discuss a Story

Well that was A LOT of information…feel like I need a nap.

But GUESS WHAT?? Now we have the pleasure of squeezing all that in a 10-minute discussion!

I know. Why put in all that work if all we need is 10 minutes worth. Simple - it's 100% worth it. All we learned through that analysis is not limited to this story or this interview. It will keep coming back to mind whenever you pick up a story or discuss the latest trend in drinks or consumer habits post-pandemic.

It's all connected. That means all the work you put in pays off because it allows you to develop an incredibly deep understanding of countless sectors of the commercial world and shine in all your interviews!

So after that little pep talk..let's get down to business on how to discuss our story and make our interviewer love us (not emotionally - just professionally).

Different Format, Different Strategies

There are many different settings in which we will be asked to demonstrate our commercial awareness. We will run through these one by one to identify the best way to stand out from other candidates and present all the work we put into our Analysis phase.

Cover Letter

Before we get into the main interview and application questions strategy, I want to give you a quick note on cover letters.

The most important thing in cover letters is to give an overview of yourself as a candidate and explain why you want to train at Firm X rather than any other firm. In addition to this, we want to show off our commercial awareness skills.

I would suggest doing this when running through why you want to train at firm X. In this section you can consider the work the firm does and the clients they work with alongside all the other points that make them *unique*.

Think about what is happening in the world at the time of writing your cover letter.

For example, you've seen in the news that Germany has a new coalition government. You know the firm you are applying to has a strong presence in Germany and advises a broad range of clients there. They also specialise in M&A, Tax and Political Law.

This is a brilliant opportunity for your show that you:

1. Researched the firm's clients and their concerns;

2. Have a genuine interest in working for them;

3. Know the work the firm does; and

4. You can apply it to *real* present-day situations

How??

Well - let's take out the example above on the German election. We know they specialise in M&A, Tax and Political Law and as we are applying here, we will assume that we are interested in these practice areas.

So we can:

1. mention their practice areas to showcase our research;

2. Mention our interest in these areas and why (trying to target the specific work the firm excels in);

3. Mention the German Election news story as an example of the fast-paced and global characteristics that attracted us to this area of law at this firm;

4. Discuss how the election can affect companies like X and Y who the firm advises in Germany and why its a problem and what work it could result in for the firm; and

5. Conclude by saying you would treasure the opportunity to take on this type of work

This should give you a good idea of how to include commercial awareness in your cover letter. Remember that the key, as always, is to target our answers to the firm we are applying to. Don't be vague. Don't copy-paste. Don't allow your answers to be used for any other firm.

Research the firm and show **why** this firm over any other one is right for **you**.

In Written Application Question

We've all seen the classic application question:

"Describe a business story you've been following. How will it impact X Firm and our clients?"

The moment you read it, tension starts running through you as you try to think about what story to pick to make the firm love you. All this is made worse when you read the "maximum 200 words" limit next to it.

Luckily we've already run through how to pick your story and how to analyse it so all that is left to do is understand how to fit our analysis in those 200 words.

The key here is to be ***clear*** and ***concise***. There is a reason why firms give you limited space to write your answer in. They want to test your ability to get your points across quickly and clearly. These are crucial skills for a lawyer and they are the points that will direct our discussion in this scenario.

The best way to answer this question is to follow a simple 3 point structure:

1. **Issue:** Explain what the story is about (30 words)

2. **Client and Firm Impact:** Explain how it will impact the firm and its clients (120 words)

3. **Conclude** Tie it all together in one line

Now that we have our structure let's take a deeper look at each of the points.

1. Issue

In the first section of our analysis, we want to show that we can explain our topic in a super concise manner. This is our time to shine from the get-go and show whœver is reading our application that we have the skills needed to make complex topics **simple**.

You can find some great examples of these in TBU's "Story in Brief" section. Our writers tend to focus on the WHO, WHAT, WHERE, WHY and HOW to structure this part of their articles. In some instances, you won't need to cover all of these but they are a useful way to get you started.

Remember you do not need to mention everything you know about the story. Many of these points will come up when you explain the impact on the firm or its clients.

I tend to re-read the story I will discuss 3-5 times before I start writing (you'll be surprised at how much we miss in the first few readings!) Then fill out the WWWWH questions above with some bullet points. This will form the basis of your issue section.

From there pick out the most relevant information and present it concisely. Here is an example for Fever-Tree:

- **Who**: Fever-Tree

- **What**: Profits hit by rising logistics costs

- **Where**: Globally

- **When:** First half of 2021

- **Why**: Rising costs in shipping and raw materials due to COVID

"Fever-Tree's profit margins fell drastically in the first half of 2021 due to rising costs of shipping and raw materials. This rise is fuelled by rapidly growing demand as COVID restrictions are lifted worldwide."

2. Client and Firm Impact

This is the key part of your answer. We want to make it VERY clear we understand how our story will affect Firm X and its Clients.

The easiest way to do this is to break down 2 or 3 key points and for each one explain how it will affect the firm and/or their clients. You do not have a lot of space to work with so you want to keep it to a few points rather than spreading yourself thin.

You can use this simple structure:

Point –> Client Impact –> Law Firm Impact

As an example, here is a list of points I picked out from our Fever-Tree story based on our Analysis:

- Rising freight/shipping costs

- Shortage of lorry drivers

- Rising inflation levels leading to new Pricing Strategies

Let's see how we can discuss their impact on the Firm and its Clients.

Impact on the Firm's Clients

Our Micro Analysis focusing on SWOT and PFF gave us some useful insights into Fever-Tree specifically. These will assist you in identifying the impact of the points we identified above on the firm's clients.

The best way to do this is to go on the firm's websites and find a few **client examples**. These are usually mentioned on their News/Press Release section or their key practice area page.

We want to find clients that operate in a similar market as our HP as these will be the ones most affected by our story. You may not find a perfect client example at times and that is fine. Think outside the box and try to find clients that may still be impacted even if they don't operate in the same market.

Note: On The Legal Update we provide collections of deals and litigation cases firms advise on divided by law firm and practice area. This can save you a lot of time at this stage of the process.

As an example, for our Fever-Tree story, we will be looking for clients operating in the drinks industry. However, we will also note down those in the logistics industry as they will be severely affected by the rising shipping prices.

Note: This step takes a little extra effort but it makes a big difference in proving you have researched the firm. Anyone can say this story will affect the firm's clients in the shipping industry but fewer people will go to the extent of mentioning them by name and outlining their specific impact.

Once you have identified these clients, make it very clear *why* and *how* they will be affected. A simple way to do this is to put yourself in their shoes. If you were the client what would you be worried about?

Taking the Shipping Costs point as an example: A client in the drinks industry will likely face the same challenges as Fever-Tree with the rising costs of shipping as it will affect its profits and cash flow at this very challenging time. This may in turn bring Company X to require loans to sustain its business, diversification of its service via a reduction of retail presence to reduce costs and renegotiation of its supply contracts.

The **How are they affected** needs to be *very* clear. You do not have a lot of space to work with. Write concise and clear so that your application reviewer sees you understand it immediately.

Impact on the Firm

We can then move on to the impact on the **Firm** part of the question. I find it helpful to connect client and firm impacts where possible. This will show your understanding of the law firm as a business affected by the same market conditions as its clients.

Our analysis needs to be **targeted**. We need to be specific with the points we pick out and explain why they would impact this particular firm. Our points may be quite broad e.g. inflation but we should try to explain their specific impact on our firm.

Try to focus on the firm's:

- Key departments

- Business structure

- Office Location

- Growth Strategy

Note: An impact can create challenges for the firm but also opportunities. In this question, the firm wants to see how you unpick the points from story and present their effects. Think strategically of any opportunities the story generates and identify any dangerous issues lying ahead.

Let's start by looking back at our PESTLE analysis which gave us a holistic view of the story. This allowed us to pick out crucial points about the market our HP operates in which gave us insights into the challenges faced by businesses globally.

An obvious example of this is the *inflation* issue we identified under our Economic heading. The Law Firm we are applying to will have to deal with this as it impacts its pricing strategies, its costs and more aspects of its business. As a quick example, many law firms are now engaging in a renewed price war by increasing salaries of junior lawyers. Many have attributed this partially to the rising level of inflation.

We can further build on this with what we found during our Trend Analysis. For example, how the growing shipping costs have led companies to follow new pricing strategies to match the rise of inflation and tackle their cash flow challenges.

Highlighting that one of our points is a *Trend* is a great way to show the depth of your research. It proves you have been following the market for a while and understand how it has developed and will continue to evolve in future.

Now that we have considered these points, we can focus on the points we identified in our **Legal Link**. This helped us identify the *legal work* that would arise from our story and the departments best placed to deal with it.

We have already identified the legal work that Rising Shipping Costs could generate even if briefly. We want this to be short and *Targeted* to our Firm.

Explain how this point will:

- generate demand for X Work (for example renegotiation of supply contracts)

- *impact* the firm by creating an *opportunity* or a *challenge*

    - To assess this, focus on the Targeting points we mentioned above including, but not limited to, the firm's strategy, office locations, key departments and business structure

    - Try to explain what this could result in (e.g. increased revenue, client demand, opportunity to take a leading position in this growing market)

- Is there anything you read that you can include?

    - E.g. A new drafting software for commercial contracts that the firm could consider to speed up their processing times etc.

Think of the Firm as *Your Business*. What would you be worried about? What opportunities could you exploit? Do they unveil any weaknesses or strengths in your business model?

For our **example** of Rising Shipping Costs, we can discuss how this could indirectly generate a positive impact for the firm due to a rush in work. Clients will want to have their logistics agreements/contracts reviewed. We can then mention how Firm X has particular expertise in drafting supply agreements for global logistics operations. Their growth strategy in Asia backed by its expertise has allowed it to gain a foothold in China which is a major hub for shipping and trade. This would allow our firm to capitalise on the growth in demand by having lawyers in the vicinity able to operate on both domestic and international matters.

Note: This point lent itself better to highlight the *opportunity* for the law firm. When discussing the Inflation point, I would focus on the *challenges* it would present to the law firm. It's important to judge the impact we consider and offer innovative conclusions to your application reviewer to help you stand out.

Time to Write

We have limited space to work with so the best strategy is to plan before you write and then re-draft several times.

For me taking each point singularly worked best by following the below structure:

1. **Point:** Rising Shipping Costs

2. **Client Impact:**Harm on profits and need for renegotiation of its supply contracts.

3. **Firm Impact:** Increase work in drafting/negotiating supply contracts.

4. **One Line Conclusion:** We do not have space to waste with a huge conclusion. One line to tie it all together is all we need. Focus on the *why* this impacts the firm and its clients.

The main part of this question is undoubtedly the **middle one**. If you can logically explain how the issue you are bringing to the table impacts the firm and its clients you will be heading in the right direction.

Following a clear structure helps you do that and showing how the firm can exploit opportunities or deal with challenges will let you stand out from other candidates.

Bonus Writing Tips

Here are some useful tips that helped me improve my writing on application forms. You will probably have heard of most of these already but it helps to check back on them when drafting an answer.

1. Prefer the active voice to the passive voice

Active: the subject dœs something eg The manager is using the computer.

Passive: the subject is done to eg The computer is being used by the manager.

Advantages of the active

- sounds more natural because the subject performs the action of the verb

- makes information more understandable by presenting it chronologically

- sounds less formal

- uses fewer words

2. Focus on what you want to say, say it and don't say more

Know your purpose and stick to it. Remove irrelevant content, from your document, clauses, paragraphs and sentences. Ask yourself, 'Do I need to say this?'

- Not: The parties cannot complete yet because the banks will not give the buyer a loan.

- But: Completion is delayed because the buyer cannot get a loan.

3. Make keywords stand out by limiting padding

Keywords contain the message. Padding words include 'of', 'the', 'which' and 'that'.

Example: the consultant's research NOT the research that the consultant conducted

4. Prefer one word to a phrase

For example, instead of: in the event that, try using: if

Or instead of: in relation to use: about

5. Avoid repeating words or ideas

Not: For the first two weeks, you must work every day of the week, from Monday to Sunday inclusive.

But: For the first two weeks, you must work on Working Days and at weekends.

Now let's move on to the big scenario…the **Interview**!

In Interview

The BIG ONE.

This is the one we prepare for the most. The one we dread the most.

The tension that rises when you look at the Partner in front of you as you try to explain what the hell is going on in your story is simply unmatched.

Luckily, there are some strategies to help us get through it with *limited* tension. (I cannot promise to make it a tense-free experience. As you will know, that is not possible).

Picking the Right Strategy

The Number One priority in this scenario is to pick the right strategy to discuss your story and stick to it.

Interviewers will usually include a **Commercial Awareness** question in interviews to test your knowledge and skills. This may take a variety of forms. For example:

- Have you been following any news lately?

- What story caught your attention in recent times?

- Is there anything in the news you think would affect our firm?

- Is there any story that would concern our clients?

The list goes on and on. Sometimes you will be given a focal point e.g. the **Firm** or the **Clients**. If that is the case, ensure you target your analysis around that point so that you tackle what the interviewer is looking for.

One of the easiest mistakes to make is to stop listening after we hear the word *story* and blast out all our research in a 10-minute monologue.

Listen to the question.

Take a sip of water to gather your thoughts and only then, get started. You will not look less professional or know-ledgeable by taking a brief pause. I cannot stress enough how important it is in delivering a confident and targeted answer.

So what strategy should we use?

I would recommend**TBU's ICTIL**. What a great acronym - so easy to pronounce right? I just remember it as I Can Touch Invisible Lions but go with whatever works for you. If you choose this mnemonic just be careful not to say it out loud in front of the partner, not sure what they would think...

Here is what ICTIL looks like.

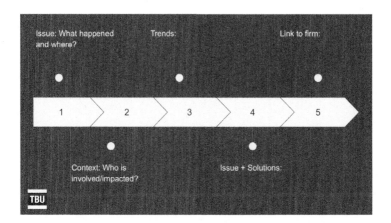

ICTIL Analysis Template

Now let's go through each of these headings to understand how you can use them to smash that interview.

ICTIL

I would suggest opening up a fresh note page with all these headings. We can then populate it with the information from our analysis. We will include additional **Target Points** to tailor our discussion to the interviewer's question depending on whether they focus on the clients, the firm, businesses in a particular industry etc.

Issue

Similar to our written application, the issue section will need to set the scene for our story. We will explain what happened and where very concisely.

Being concise in this section is crucial because it shows your ability to convey complicated stories quickly and clearly. That is a great skill to show your interviewer because as a lawyer you will be expected to do this regularly for clients.

Making the complex simple is a must-have skill for a lawyer so let's show our Interviewer we have what it takes.

Two points to check off here in 1 or 2 sentences tops:

1. What happened?

2. Where?

Objective: Show ability to convey complicated stories clearly and concisely.

As an **example**, for Fever-Tree we would say:

Fever-Tree's profits have been hit heavily by the rising costs in logistics. These were driven by a spike in global demand as COVID restrictions eased.

Super simple. We say what happened i.e. Fever-Tree's profits being hit and where it happened i.e. Globally (no need to be overly specific - just helps put the story in context).

Context

Speaking of context, the Context section of our strategy mainly involves discussing the Parties involved and/or impacted.

Objective: Show our understanding of how a Story can affect different parties and our ability to prioritise impacted parties. This is crucial in being a lawyer and recognising issues before our clients to provide efficient solutions.

The easiest way to plan this is to make a list of all the parties you think will be impacted by this story. Next to them, we will write in bullet point format why and how they will affected.

Here are the best resources to use from our analysis:

- For the **Subject** of our Story (Fever-Tree) look at our SWOT Analysis

125

- For **Competitors** (those operating in the same market) check Porter's Five Forces

- For **Parties outside the Industry** check the PESTLE Analysis. Try to go through each of the sections and think of any parties that stand out. For example, the local government for the Political heading, business in other sectors (e.g. logistics) for Economical, tech startups for Technological etc.

- For **Law Firms** and entities in the Legal Sector check the Legal Link section

Target Points:

This is where you start preparing your Target Points to tailor your answer to the Interviewers Question. You can pick out the impacts on a particular industry under the 2nd and 3rd points and focus on the Firm and its Clients under the 4th point.

There is no need to go too in-depth on the Law Firms & Clients as the last section of ICTIL is wholly focused on them. Use this part to introduce them if you are lacking other parties to mention. If you are struggling for space, focus on other parties and tackle the Firm & Clients later on.

Once you have your parties, note down why and how they are involved & impacted.

So for example:

Businesses in the Logistics Industry are:

- **Involved**: Due to the growing demand for their services.

- **Impacted**: By higher profits due to rising prices, struggle to satisfy all requests, potential litigation claims for failing to meet requirements.

You can easily end up with a list of 10 or more parties involved from any given story. If that is the case, be sure to prioritise your choices. Pick out 2-4 parties including your Subject who would be particularly impacted.

Prioritising parties will show your interviewer your complete understanding of the story. You can pick out key points and turn them into the reasoning for addressing issues.

As a lawyer, you will work under stressful conditions and being able to **Prioritise** is crucial to providing a great service to the client.

There may be 10 things on your desk but 3 of them will need to be done before the other 7. Show you know how to pick those 3 things in your interview indirectly by prioritising your parties.

A simple way to rank is by looking at how many points they have next to them. If tech startups only have 1 point in the Impact column whereas Logistics Businesses have 3 you will know that the latter must be mentioned.

If they have a similar amount of points, think critically about which one can be most useful for your analysis. For example, say we were asked how a story we read impacts the firm's clients. We would look at the Firm we are applying to, where they operate and who their clients are. From our research, we know they act for businesses in the Drinks Industry and do not have a physical presence nor advise the Local Government of Country X.

If that were the case, we would mention Parties in the Drinks Industry over the Local Government of Country X to tailor our analysis to the firm we are applying to.

Trends

Trends are back! We love them and we love the formula we got from our Trends Analysis section:

History of the News Story + Matching Stories + Look to the Future

So let's look back through that section to pick out the ones we will discuss. For ease, the ones we got for Fever-Tree were:

1.   Fever-Tree's Sales Struggles

2.   Inflation

3.   Price rises plans

We already have our list of key points which we made during our Analysis phase. This will save us a lot of time in preparing for this interview section. All we have to do is lift the points from that list and place them in our Question prep.

In this section of our discussion, we want to outline how these trends link to the story.

A great way to make the discussion flow is to start the Trend phase via the last Party you mention in the Context phase. For example, if the last Party we discuss is a Logistics Business, we could link this up with the rising cost of inflation or the spike in demand that led many companies to rethink their price plans.

There is no need to force a link but usually, it should be fairly easy to find one to link your discussion as they are based on the story we selected. If you are struggling to find one you can always just start this section with something like: "And this Story highlights some interesting trends in the market such as…".

Once we have opened up our Trends discussion, we can go on to discuss each one of our trends. To do this you may want to follow this simple structure:

1. Trend: Which one? *Inflation*

2. Trend Effect: What impact/effect is it having? *Raising prices globally. Reducing the value of savings.*

3. Link to the Story: How does it fit into our story? *Rising price plans by parties in the industry, their suppliers and logistics businesses as the global economy exits COVID restrictions*

Note: If the question asks how our story impact a certain market or industry you can tie this into this part of the discussion. Particularly under headings 2 and 3 above. Mention the industry and explain how it impacts them.

Issues and Solutions

In this section, we want to highlight the Challenges and Issues raised by the story and propose any solutions.

An **Issue** is simply something that could raise challenges for the firm, its clients or a specific market industry. A good point to start from is our Threats and Weaknesses section in the SWOT Analysis. We can build on these problems with Porter's Five Forces if we want to determine subject-specific issues or PESTLE to identify broader industry issues.

As an example, in our story about Fever-Tree, an issue could be the booming prices demanded by logistics businesses.

Once we have identified the issue we can explain who it impacts and how. In this story, it would be businesses operating in the Drinks industry like Fever-Tree and beyond that any business that relies on logistics. They need logistics to supply and deliver their product. Higher logistics prices directly affect these companies' profit margins and their success in the industry which could result in severe cuts to remain profitable.

Now that we have explained the issue we can move on to the Solution.

Finding Solutions to problems is a lawyer's job description. Law Firms want to hire people that can take the initiative and come up with innovative solutions to complex problems.

That is why we included this section in our discussion. We need to show the interviewer we *have* this skill.

To do this, we can start by looking at our issue (in this case the booming prices demanded by logistics businesses) and critically think of what could either solve or reduce it.

To plan this, try to put your issue at the centre of a page of A4 and start **brainstorming**. Jot down anything that comes to mind without overthinking it.

It helps to think of solutions from the perspective of:

- a business (your HP & others in the same industry and beyond)

- a law firm

- local government

Depending on the depth of your issue, you will then be left with quite a sizeable list of solutions that we can narrow down.

We are aiming for 2 or a maximum of 3 solutions per issue. Any more than that would take too long to explain.

Once we have selected our solutions, we can run through them in our discussion via this simple strategy:

1. **Link to Issue** (What issue is this solution for?)

2. **Mention the perspective** (e.g. business, law firm - helps give context to your ideas and shows your understanding of different parties' concerns)

3. **What is the solution?** (Renegotiate supply contract to decrease prices)

4. **How would it solve or reduce the issue?** (Potentially lower prices and reduce the impact on HP's profit margins)

Link to Firm

As we are applying to a law firm, we must link our story to them, their business and their clients.

The question from the partner may ask to focus on this. If so, give this section more space in your discussion and reduce other sections e.g. issues relating to other businesses or the government (unless they are similar to their clients!).

If the question doesn't specifically mention the firm or its clients, still address this section. It makes your answer relevant to them and shows you went a step further in your analysis as 99% of the time, news articles will not mention the impact on law firms or their clients. This shows your initiative in reaching new solutions and willingness to learn about challenges in the legal industry.

Revisit our **Legal Link** section in our analysis and use it to make this section a breeze. Try to look for similar tasks that lawyers would be expected to take on. You can then try to match these with the examples that law firms usually give under the practice area pages on their websites.

Remember we want to focus on the practice areas the firm we are applying to is particularly strong in or areas they are looking to strengthen for the future. This will show we are keen on joining them and are not just copy-pasting our answers.

Choose 2 or 3 points from the story and run through these. Show how they Impact the firm's Clients or how they Impact the Firm itself by way of Opportunities and/or Challenges.

Addressing Improv Questions

The interviewer may hit you at any point (not physically!) with a *surprise question*.

We need to be ready for these. They are a strategy used to test our knowledge. The interviewer wants to verify you know what you are talking about as opposed to simply memorising a script.

To prepare for this, I used to do a final brainstorm following my entire analysis and discussion planning phase. In it, I would focus on areas that could naturally lead to additional questions.

A good way to do this is to run through your analysis and planned discussion above and for each section ask yourself:

- is there anything I would ask or want to hear more of?

- does this make sense?

- could I add more detail to this?

- how would this impact other parties?

Assess your analysis and discussion and plot down these questions in your brainstorm. Then add your answers in bullet point form under them. You will then have a *cheatsheet* to smash the most likely improvisation questions and feel confident in your interview.

Note: Sometimes you will be caught off guard by a question you did not prepare for. If that is the case, do not worry. Take a sip of water and plan your answer. You know your story inside out. Use what you learnt through your analysis and discussion to present a well-reasoned answer to your interviewer. Most times, there is no right or wrong. It's about testing how you present information clearly and concisely.

Now let's take a look at another classic scenario, the Case Study.

In Case Study

The Classic Case Study. It wouldn't; be an assessment centre without it!

I found this part of the application process particularly challenging. You are given limited time usually 1 hour to go through a block of notes on the case, formulate your answer to the questions and then discuss them in front of a partner (just to add a bit of stress to the whole thing!).

And if that's not enough, we now have to think about commercial awareness in our answer??

I know…it may sound like an unnecessary detail. Something we should put at the bottom of our priority list while we tackle the actual answers to the case study.

However, Commercial Awareness is everywhere and we should assess its impact on this basis. (Yes - this book is just a bit biased but stay with me, it will be worth it).

In the First Chapter, we discussed how we should aim to be *CEOs with High Levels of Awareness* to develop our commercial awareness skills.

This notion comes particularly handy in the case of studies as quite frequently you will be asked to advise a specific business on a series of issues it is facing.

In a case study that stuck with me, I was asked to advise a bike shop. To summarise their issues:

- their storefront was damaged;

- their sales were decreasing due to lower-priced products offered by the competition;

- they were facing complaints from employees; and

- had a growing number of returns from customers due to faulty products

The questions at the end of the pack asked us to address these issues and present them to a partner in the form of advice acting as if *they were the client*.

All these questions are testing your commercial awareness. They focus on different issues and different impacts to the business to test how *you* address them and present an effective strategy to your client.

So how do we go about showing our commercial awareness in this situation?

The first step is to **unpick the story** we are given with reference to the questions. Find all the important information you need and highlight it with different colours if you can. (If not possible use your own code e.g. circle, underline or put in brackets the same points).

I used to highlight our HP (the Bike Shop) in yellow and problems in different colours. All points relating to the same problem would be in the same colour.

For example, Sales Decreasing = Problem 1 (Highlight in Red). Competitors releasing new eco bikes for half the price of our HP's bikes = Information related to Problem 1 (also Highlight in Red).

Now that we have our information let's start planning our discussion in bullet points for each question. This is when your Commercial Awareness comes into play.

A question may be as simple as *"What should the bike shop do to address its decreasing sales?"*.

That is quite a broad question and it is subtly testing your Commercial Awareness. The interviewer wants you to explain what is causing the problem, what solutions there are and in what order the bike shop should address them.

You can start listing the problems you highlighted in your reading and for each one identify why it is an issue for your HP.

In this case, we know the decreasing sales are the **main problem** but there will be several contributing factors to this.

For example:

- The decreasing quality of their products

- Cheaper products offered by competitors

- Decrease in popularity of bikes

- Remote Working reducing the need to commute

- And the list goes on!

Mentioning these as an introduction to your HP's issue will show your full understanding of the problem at hand and lead you into discussing the solutions.

The solutions may or may not be available from your reading. The case study may throw in some *hints* for you to solve these issues. For example, they might tell you that the bike shop has considered adopting cheaper prices, focusing on online sales or offering a rental service via membership for workers commuting only 2 or 3 days of the week.

If they offer you these hints, pick them out and explain *how* they could solve the decreasing sales issue. This will show your attention to detail and ability to work with real facts to develop innovative solutions. (Which is what Lawyers are expected to do!)

Speaking of finding innovative solutions, you can take this a step further by going beyond what you find in your reading. This is where your commercial awareness truly comes into play. You need to think of ways to help your client and these may not always be handed to you on the notes.

The third step focuses on **Planning our discussion** to **Prioritise our answer**. I failed to do this in one of the Assessment Centres I attended and it was one of the points mentioned in my constructive feedback.

Your clients want a clear answer. They want to know what needs to be done to solve their problem. If there are multiple things to do, they need to know which ones take priority.

A lawyer needs to be a problem fixer. The client comes to us with a problem, we sort it and go back to them with an easy solution(s).

That is what we want to show our interviewer. A solution that makes sense for the client. To do this, we need to list the issues and their respective solutions in order of priority.

To do this try to consider:

- Which ones are most heavily affecting the business?

- Which ones can be solved "easily"?

- Which ones cannot wait?

A useful tool to assist with this is the Eisenhower Matrix. This is a simple tool with four different squares for you to categorise tasks in and we can adapt it to the **prioritisation** section of our discussion.

	Urgent	Not Urgent
Important	**Do it** Things with clear deadlines and consequences for not taking immediate action. Examples: · Finishing a client project · Submitting a draft article · Responding to some emails · Picking up your sick kid from school	**Schedule it** Activities without a set deadline that bring you closer to your goals. Easy to procrastinate on. Examples: · Strategic planning · Professional development · Networking · Exercise
Not Important	**Delegate it** Things that need to be done, but don't require your specific skills. Busy work. Examples: · Uploading blog posts · Scheduling · Responding to some emails · Meal prep	**Delete it** Distractions that make you feel worse afterward. Can be ok but only in moderation. Examples: · Social media · Watching TV · Video games · Eating junk food

You may find some problems can be solved with just a few actions but may not lead to any change for the client e.g. changing the colour of pens to blue to match their branding.

This is important but is it as urgent as finding a solution to the decreasing demand for our HP's bikes? The latter will probably take priority because if they have no demand they have no sales and consequently, no profits which means their business may go bust.

Once you know what takes priority, explain *why* that is the case. This shows the interviewer you thought about it and are not just listing problems & solutions at random.

A simple structure is:

1. Problem

2. Solution

3. Why tackle this now? What effect does this have?

Remember that the HP at the centre of the case study is your focus. We need to show our interviewer that we can understand what worries our HP, what opportunities excite them and what solutions would work best for them.

Showing real concern for our HP and providing a clear explanation as to why we should go for options A and B before C and D will make a huge difference in your interview.

Focus on this, do your best and smash that interview.

In Lunch with Partners

Oof. This is the tricky one.

Not only do we have the stress of eating at a table with partners but now we need to show off our commercial awareness too?!

I know, I know. It seems a bit too much but trust me - it's ok once you know how to do this.

The trickiest part of this scenario is given by what I like to refer to as **Indirect Commercial Awareness**. The idea is simple. We may not be asked *direct* commercial awareness questions such as: "Tell me about a story from the news". So how do we go about showing off our commercial awareness?

In these scenarios, law firms want to test your social abilities. They want to see how you act in a non-professional environment. Can you hold the conversation? Can you bring interesting talking points to the table? Can you engage and bounce off others?

A massive part of being a lawyer is the *social* aspect. We must be able to interact with colleagues and clients seamlessly and build a network that allows us to bring in new clients and cultivate current ones.

Being able to show commercial awareness is crucial because it allows you to bring interesting points to the table and bounce off others. How many times have you been at a dinner table and someone started talking about something they heard of in the news? Quite often right?

It's a very common conversation starter and if you are ready to jump on whatever topic is brought up you'll impress the partners with your commercial awareness and social skills.

As mentioned, you may not be directly asked this but you need to be able to weave commercial awareness into the discussion. This is where our holistic understanding of commercial awareness pays off the most because this is the scenario we can prepare for the least. We must be able to *improvise*.

There are two ways you can bring in commercial awareness:

1. **Proactively**: Start the conversation yourself with a topic that is on the news

2. **Reactively**: Link to a story that someone at the table mentioned

Both are great as they allow you to input your innovative points in the conversations. Let's take a look at how both can work.

Proactively

Has there been anything in the news in the week of your lunch that stood out to you? We want a topic that most people will have heard about to spark a bigger conversation rather than a 1 on 1.

Make sure you read up on it so that you can bring quite a few different points up and engage in the conversation as much as possible.

Try to think of how it could affect the firm and its clients too to ask specific questions to the partners e.g. so is this something you think could affect clients in your Real Estate department?

Once you have your selected story it's as simple as mentioning it wherever appropriate. Don't force it. Instead try to link it to what is being discussed if possible. That is why it's important to have a range of stories at hand. It increases your chances of linking the story to the current topic.

So pick out a good number of stories you are quite confident on (for example 3-5). I would also suggest having some unique side stories to link to those to help you bring something unique to the table and positively surprise the partners with your knowledge. Try to look through "related stories" sections on news websites to pick these out.

In my experience, the discussion will tend to cover a bit about the applicants at the table, a bit about the partners and some general discussion. In the third section, you want to bring your story to the table.

For example, if the partners mention they have been very busy in real estate lately, you can say that you saw in the news this spike in demand for house sales driven by the stamp duty holiday and ask them how they coped.

This shows A) Your Knowledge B) Your Interest and C) Your Social Skills.

Lots of good points for you to stand out from the other applicants.

Note: Don't feel that you have to force through your points first at all costs. Listening to others and linking up to their points to introduce yours can be equally valuable to showcase your listening and communication skills.

Reactively

On the other side, we have a reactionary strategy. Here we are playing off what is thrown to the table by others to add value to the conversation.

Our additions should ideally be new and unique. The more we focus on these two principles the more we will stand out throughout the lunch.

The tactic is deceivingly simple. Listen to what others are saying and add to it.

The fact is we need to have quite a broad knowledge base to be able to do this. Indeed, this is where all the time we have put into developing our commercial awareness truly bears fruit.

Every story we spent time analysing and practised rehearsing is inherently connected to all the other stories floating around the news.

The links we trained our mind to build particularly during the Trends Section will prove extremely useful. We connected so many stories to the same trend. That is precisely what we want to do here.

The stories we picked out for our Proactive section will also come in handy here as they will be the most likely stories to be discussed.

So how do we put this into action?

Well..the obvious number 1 skill here is **listening**. Being a good listener will help you pick out points you can tie your discussion to and show off your attention to detail.

The best way to do this is to remember what someone said and link it back into your discussion.

The second part is to create a **link** and **add value** to what is being said. That means building on the points already on the table with something new and hopefully interesting.

For example, the partner points out how the UK's Energy Crisis may have something to do with Russia's ambitions to deliver a new gas pipeline.

You can create a **link** by saying you read into that too and saw how this crisis could be an opportunity for Russia to pressure through the approval of the pipeline by controlling the supply in a market filled with demand.

You can then mention how the drop in wind energy can also be to blame and how numerous industries such as Health, Steel, Meat are struggling as they all rely on CO_2 for various reasons. For example, the NHS needs it for their surgeries.

Then **ask** them a question to continue the conversation. For example, "do you think that this is something that could affect your clients who heavily rely on a stable supply of electricity and gas as part of their business structure?".

You can make this question even more specific if you know the firm has clients operating in the industries mentioned above and if the partner you are talking to advises them.

For example: "I saw your Corporate department works with many clients operating in the Energy Industry such as X and Y. Do you think this will heavily impact them both in the short and long term?"

This sort of question shows you:

1. researched what they (the partners) do;

2. researched their clients and what issues they may face;

3. think strategically about problems by considering both short and long term implications; and

4. Can keep a conversation going with an interesting open question

These are all great points. They prove you have the skills to shine as a lawyer and become a valuable asset to the firm!

Learning Points

Different scenarios, Different strategies

We need to use different strategies depending on the scenario we are facing. They all hold unique challenges therefore it's important to run through our tactics before you start planning your answers.

There isn't much point in summarising these as important details will inevitably be missed out. Take the time to go through what we discussed above, it will be worth it!

Build a complete commercial awareness

Putting in the time to research stories, taking notes and building trend tables will help you develop a holistic commercial awareness. This will be crucial in answering unexpected questions in interviews, partner lunches and case study presentations!

Also, it will make you feel great to know what's going on in the world and be able to discuss it with anyone!

Action Points

Practice, Practice, Practice

In the end, this is what it comes to. Every time you practice your answers (both oral and written) you increase your odds of doing well.

We can talk about how to do something as much as we want but this is the part that makes the real difference. Practice your analysis, your communication and your discussion because they will be very helpful even beyond the application stage.

These are skills I use today. I still analyse stories, I still build trend links and discuss them with whoever wants to. And I love it.

Thank you

Thank you for taking the time to read this book. I know at times it may have felt like an endless flow of thoughts spat on paper. That's probably because I wanted to capture all I learnt throughout the years of applications and ultimately securing a Training Contract.

I truly hope this helps you even just a tiny bit. You have what it takes to succeed so don't give up on your dream.

I'm here for anything so feel free to reach out to me via LinkedIn at any point!

Much love

Ludo

Printed in Great Britain
by Amazon

79883305R00088